# ClothesCare

### SECRETS OF THE PROFESSIONALS

A quality wardrobe demands quality care. CLOTHESCARE offers important tips on:

- Getting the perfect fit—whether custom-made or ready-made
- How to maintain your wardrobe—brushing, laundering, ironing, and pressing
- Stain removal and emergency repairs
- How to get proper alterations from your tailor
- How to fold, pack, and store your clothes
- Care and preservation of all your leather goods

From the finest techniques to the unique and surprising advice on special problems, CLOTHESCARE is the one—the only—clothing guide you'll ever need to preserve and enjoy your fine apparel.

# ClothesCare

## SECRETS OF THE PROFESSIONALS

by
James Wagenvoord
and
Fiona St. Aubyn

Illustrations by Sandra Forrest

A WALLABY BOOK
Published by Pocket Books
New York

Another *Original* publication of WALLABY BOOKS

 A Wallaby Book published by
POCKET BOOKS, a division of Simon & Schuster, Inc.
1230 Avenue of the Americas, New York, N.Y. 10020

ISBN: 0-671-52370-8

First Wallaby Books trade paperback printing March, 1985

10  9  8  7  6  5  4  3  2  1

Created and Produced by
James Wagenvoord Studio, Inc.
340 East 66th Street
New York, N.Y. 10021

EDITOR-IN-CHIEF
James Wagenvoord

EXECUTIVE EDITOR
Patricia Coen

DESIGN DIRECTOR
Sandra Forrest

ASSISTANT EDITOR
Judd Howard

DESIGN ASSOCIATE
Rebecca Adams

## Acknowledgments

This book could not have been made without the many people who generously gave us their time and insight. We are especially grateful to:

Mark Fairweather; Frank Hurd; Mademoiselle Elise Gaubert; Thomas Hill; Odile Barbiere; Nanny Chadwyck-Healey; Maureen Gavin; Sava Rasic Harris; Bill Pashley; Angus Cundey; Albert Villeneuve; John Lobb; Mary and Piers St. Aubyn; Ana and Richard Nevill; John Woolf; Stanley Ager; David Rumage; Toby Weller-Foley; Tom Lewis; Jennifer Plunket; Julia and Peregrine Chadwyck-Healey; Richard and Linda Robinson; Mary Wright; Sylvie Barillot; Juanita Coen; Henry A. Echeverria; Dorothy Shubert.

We would also like to express our appreciation to the following firms and organizations for their cooperation during the making of this book:

Henry Poole & Co.; Sullivan Wooley & Co.; Louis Vuitton; The Royal Ballet Company; Mark of Knightsbridge; Maxwell Croft Furs; Austin Reed of Regent Street-Knightsbridge Branch; John Lobb, Ltd.; Guillaume; Scope; Harrods, Ltd.; The London Library; Kensington and Central Library; John Palmer, Ltd.; Kent of Lond; Roncastle London, Ltd.; the Kiwi Polish Company, Ltd.; Good Housekeeping Magazine; Marley Hodgson, Trafalgar Ltd; Neighborhood Cleaners Association; Leather Industries of America, Inc.; Euramerica, Inc.; The Fabric Research Institute.

Table of Contents

# BODY LANGUAGE

## First It Has To Fit

The right fit is the key to clothescare. Every article of clothing is designed to fit the body in a specific fashion, and clothes that don't conform to your contours won't last as long or look as well as they should. If your clothes are too tight, the strain placed on them will, without question, shorten their wearing life. And if they are too large, wrinkles and rumples will dictate more handling (ironing and pressing) than they were designed to withstand. Clothescare begins in the department stores, the clothing shops, and at the tailor's.

## Recognizing Quality

**Classics:** The best clothes are timeless. Their cut and design cannot be improved upon and the quality of the fabrics is such that, with care, the garment will last for years and years. The best clothes finally fall apart rather than out of fashion. These clothes have been dubbed 'Classics' because they are both traditional and long lasting. Classics can come in many shapes, from a Savile Row suit to a pair of designer jeans, and they inspire copies at every price level of the ever-expanding ready-to-wear market.

There are three ways of buying a suit. You can choose off-the-peg (rack), semi-custom, or custom-made suits. The difference between them lies in price, quality and fit. The more a suit is tailored to meet your needs, the more it's going to cost. Ready-made suits are the least expensive because they're altered to fit you after they're made. Semi-custom-made suits cost more because they are cut from a standard pattern that is altered to suit your measurements before the suit is made up. Subsequent alterations are usually made after it's sewn together. But the Rolls Royce of tailoring is the custom-made suit. The pattern is cut to the shape, size, and requirements of the individual and alterations are carried out during two or three fittings as your suit is fitted piece by piece to your body.

**The Bespoke Trade:** London's Savile Row has long been synonymous with the English 'bespoke' or custom-made tailoring industry. The street lies between the two great shopping areas of Regent Street and Bond Street, and in the early 1800s Henry Poole, one of the city's leading tailors, first opened up shop here. Founded in 1806 as *Henry Poole and Company*, it is now called *Henry Poole Sullivan Woolley*. They continue to make high quality suits for men and women at prices that start around £510 (approximately $800). The top end of the ready-to-wear market is about £350 (approximately $575).

The firm's part owner and managing director, Angus Cundey, says, "Sadly, the bespoke trade accounts for only a very small percent of the population, but once a customer has had a custom-made suit, he never goes back to ready-to-wear. He

*"The contemporary man does not need to have a morning coat, a frock coat, a dress coat and a dinner jacket (and the appropriate trousers, shirts and shoes) as he did in the 1900s. Nor must the contemporary woman possess morning costumes, walking costumes, afternoon costumes, tea gowns, motoring outfits and evening dresses."*

— Alison Lurie,
*The Language of Clothes*

finds ready-made suits uncomfortable and he misses the detail and finish of custom-made clothes. Ladies come to us because they like a tailored look and because we provide a choice of fine clothes that aren't available in retail stores."

**Ready-to-Wear:** The history of ready-to-wear is the history of 20th century fashion. It has turned from a privilege for an elite few into a vast industry that is influenced by a host of different designers from all over the world and popularized by different segments of society. At the turn-of-the-century, fashion was still in the hands of the haute couturier and bespoke tailor who made clothing for those wealthy few who could afford their prices. High society and couturiers dictated fashion, and stylish Americans and Europeans went to Paris, which was for centuries the center of fashion, to buy clothes. It wasn't until after World War I that the ready-to-wear boom really began. When it did, the United States led the way in production and marketing.

Because ready-to-wear garments are mass-produced it's important to check how the garment is finished. You should also look at the label to see what it's made of (see page 26). Natural fabrics carry more status and are more comfortable to wear than less expensive man-made ones, but synthetic fibers are more durable. Synthetics tend to shine after prolonged wear instead of wearing into holes as natural fabrics do. A blend of natural and synthetic fibers — such as wool and polyester — is a strong and practical combination.

## Jackets and Coats

**Jackets:** Although they vary in cut, tailored women's jackets are constructed almost the same way as men's jackets, and the quality checks are the same.

**Collar and Lapels:** It's important that the collar and lapels gently roll—without looking pressed—onto the jacket. Turn up the collar to see how it's attached; small even stitches are a sign that it has been hand-sewn and is therefore of higher quality. On a man's suit, the stitching around the edges of the lapels should be discreet and look as though it has been done by hand, as on a custom-made suit.

**Interlinings and Facings:** The interlining in the lapels, chest and shoulders help give the jacket its body and shape. The best interlining is made up of different layers of canvas, horsehair, and felt that are sewn into the jacket. As the tailor sews, he gently rolls the layers of fabric in his hand to give life to the finish and stop the suit from looking cardboard smooth. The interlinings in ready-made jackets are fused to the suit fabric before it is sewn together by machine. Bespoke tailors say you can tell the difference after six months, when ready-made jackets begin to look slightly limp in comparison to the custom-made garment.

**Seams:** The raw edges along the seams should be oversewn by machine. Check that there is at least two to three inches inlay in the back and side seams so that the jacket can be let out when necessary. *Henry Poole*'s clients wear jackets that are over 50 years old because the original tailors put enough inlay in the seams to allow alterations.

**Linings:** Better jackets are fully lined, usually with rayon or silk. Check to see that the sleeve lining is stitched securely at the armhhole to the body of the jacket. Don't be afraid of colorful linings. A contrasting color can enhance a jacket—a burgundy lining looks sensational in a dark blue blazer and a contrasting shade or patterned

*"There are certain ways you can tell if a garment has been hand-made rather than mass-produced. Take the traditional, classic four-holed button. A machine-sewn button will have two parallel lines of stitching; a hand-sewn button will have stitching crossed over on the button. No one has yet invented a machine that can do that."*

— Bill Pashley

lining brightens up a suit jacket.

**Buttons and Buttonholes:** On a custom-made jacket the buttonholes are hand-stitched and backed with canvas. The row of buttons on the sleeves have real buttonholes, not false ones. On a man's suit, there's a small tab behind the lapel buttonhole to hold the stem of a flower in place. The buttons are, of course, all sewn on by hand. When buying ready-to-wear jackets, make sure the buttons are securely sewn and check to see whether they are made of bone or plastic.

**Fabrics:** Reject anything that looks cheap, such as obvious polyester. Reject any garment with a pattern that doesn't match up at the seams. The stripes on a suit jacket should line up with the stripes on the suit trousers or skirt.

To find out if the material will crease easily, take a sleeve in your hands and twist it hard for 12 to 15 seconds, then let it go. If the sleeve springs back without a wrinkle, the garment won't crush easily. If it stays crumpled, be prepared for a lot of extra work if you buy that particular item.

**Coats:** The better the fabric, the warmer the coat will be, and the longer it will last. A good quality coat is unlikely to look shabby after one season's wearing. Avoid fussy details such as extra pockets, gaudy buttons or buckles — these tend to brand a garment as cheap. Follow the quality check for jackets.

**Fur:** It's better to buy the very best quality of a less expensive type of fur than to buy a poor quality example of a very costly fur. The quality checks are different for each type of fur you buy, but the overall beauty of any fur lies in its natural sheen and how fine and silken it feels when you run your hand down it. Most fur has a top wool (the fur you see) and an under wool (the darker, thicker fur underneath). The top wool must not be too long or it will become spiky. The under wool should be close and dense, but not so dense that it will become matted. If you part the fur, you should not be able to see where the different skins have been sewn together (known as the 'drops') to make the coat.

The lifespan of a fur depends on how well it's treated and the durability of the fur itself. All furs change color with age. Reddish furs tend to go a deeper color while dark browns become paler. Mink that has been dyed will gradually fade back to its original color, and as the true color of each skin begins to show up the coat will look patchy. Fine quality natural mink will fade evenly all over.

## Trousers and Jeans

**Trousers:** Make sure there is enough excess material to let out the crotch if necessary, and that the waistband is reinforced to keep it from rolling over the top of your belt. In men's suits there should be a second button inside the fly, just below the waist button, for more support and a better fit. This additional button also takes some of the strain off the waist button. The fly zipper should be plastic, not metal, and it should match the color of the suit.

**Jeans:** The word denim is derived from 'de Nimes,' meaning 'of Nimes,' a city in France where denim work trousers were made for farmers and sailors in the last century. In the mid-1800s Levi Strauss, a Bavarian immigrant, started selling denims to cowboys and miners passing through San Francisco, and they were regarded as working trousers for the next 100 years—until they came into their own as both practical and fashionable in the 1960s. Their durability is still an essential part of their style. Look for a strong metal zipper, double stitching on seams, pockets and flies, and reinforced stress points on pocket corners, the zipper base and belt loops.

## Dresses and Skirts

**Dresses:** "In the old days," according to top British designer Bill Pashley, "all couture dresses were lined, the buttons, and zippers, hems and facings were hand-sewn and even the seams were oversewn by hand. Today the most expensive dress can be unlined and the facings are unlikely to be attached by hand." So whatever your price range, make sure the seams are oversewn to prevent frayed edges and that the zipper matches the dress and is concealed in the seam. There should be no puckers where the sleeve joins the shoulder nor where the pockets are attached to the dress.

Uneven hemlines indicate shoddy workmanship, and a hem looks better if you can't see the machine stitches on the outside. If the dress has horizontal stripes, the stripes should run around the bottom of the hem without falling off it.

**Skirts:** Check the zipper and seams as you would when choosing a dress. A winter skirt should be fully lined with matching lining, and its waistband should be reinforced. A generous hem balances the skirt and allows you to raise or lower it as you wish.

## Underwear

During the 19th century, the term 'linen' was synonymous with gentlemen's under-

*"People should select colors that go with their skins. And elderly women should not wear grass green, or royal blue, or purple, or any hard color that needs a faultless complexion. Swarthy skin always looks better in colors that have red or yellow in them...Pink and orchid are often very becoming to older women; pale blue or yellow to those with fair skin. Because a woman is no longer young is no reason why she should wear perpetual black—unless she is fat."*

*—Emily Post, 1922*

wear and this old-fashioned term is still sometimes used today. Linen was considered superior to, and more luxurious than, cotton, although gentlemen wore silk underwear with their evening clothes. Women wore silk lingerie both during the day and in the evening. However, since the advent of rayon in the 1920s, women have been able to enjoy the smooth, sensuous feeling of silk without spending the small fortune that silk requires.

**Underpants:** Cotton underpants should be worn by women who suffer from any form of cystitis as cotton is a natural fiber and is porous, absorbent, and able to breathe. Men's cotton underpants, and the more durable cotton blend underpants, are more comfortable in warm weather than men's nylon briefs.

## Shirts and Sweaters

**Shirts:** Fabrics may be natural, man-made or blends. Natural fibers are both cool and comfortable but tend to crumple more easily than synthetic shirts. But synthetic shirts can't breathe and may become too hot. The best of both worlds lies in polyester-and-cotton blends which are as cool as cotton and as wrinkle-free as synthetics.

**Sweaters:** The best sweaters are knitted as a whole, with the sleeves properly set in, not sewn together from separate pieces.

## Boots and Shoes

The skin and hides vary to suit the type of boots or shoes you buy and the tanning process varies with different types of leather. Hand-stitched shoes last longer and wear better. Leather linings, leather heels and leather soles are all signs of quality.

# Sizing Yourself

Even if your budget doesn't allow for custom-made suits, the rules for a good fit remain the same. And an important point to remember when trying on any clothes is that you must relax and let your body settle into its normal posture to get an honest fit. Unless your posture is usually ramrod stiff, don't stand up perfectly straight, no matter what the tailor says.

## Jackets/Men

**Collar:** The jacket collar should lie flat against the back of your neck with about half an inch of shirt collar showing above it. If you have ridges or puckers at the back of the jacket, the collar needs to be removed and reattached. Trying to alter the problem with the collar in place will only produce more bumps and tucks.

**Shoulders:** Make sure the left and right shoulders are evenly balanced. Sometimes the right shoulder is lower than the left, which causes a lopsided look and affects the balance of the jacket.

**Sleeves:** Show about half an inch of shirt cuff beneath the sleeves, which should stop approximately five inches from the tip of your thumb.

**Chest and Back:** Good tailoring combines elegance with comfort. A jacket should be loose enough across the shoulders to allow you to move your arms freely. Horizontal ripples across the back mean that it's too tight. A vertical crease down the back means that it's too loose, causing the lapels to sag in front.

**Buttons:** The buttons and buttonholes should hang directly opposite each other. Tradition dictates that you button only one button on your jacket — the top one if it's a two-button suit; the middle one if it has three buttons. A faint X-shaped crease should extend out from the button. A distinct crease means that the jacket is too tight around the middle.

**Pockets:** It's important that you transfer all the bits and pieces that you normally carry around with you into the pockets of your new jacket so that they can be taken into consideration when the tailor makes alterations. "But the more you carry in your pockets, the more you spoil the line of your suit," warns Angus Cundey. "You can make an extremely elegant suit for a customer, and he starts putting wallets, pipes, and cigarette packets in his pockets and a lot of the elegance disappears."

Ready-to-wear suits have extra cloth in the lining to hold the bulk carried in the breast pockets. Savile Row tailors, however, make separate pockets to fit each item the customer carries. They make pockets of all sizes to hold wallets, cigarette lighters, combs or credit cards. These custom-made pockets keep items easily at hand in addition to giving the jacket a much slimmer line than one carry-all pocket permits.

**Length:** The best way to find the right length is to let your arms hang straight by your sides. Curl your fingers. The hem of the jacket should fit into that curl.

### Jackets/Women:

The guidelines for choosing a well-fitting woman's jacket are virtually the same as for a man's jacket. Remember that the collar and lapels should lie flat and that the jacket mustn't fit too snugly across the chest or buttocks.

### Trousers/Men:

**Waist:** Should come fairly high up on your body, slightly below your navel. It should fit snugly with just enough room for you to slip your hand between you and the waistband.

**Seat:** Must be smooth and flat but not tight.

**Crotch:** Have it altered if it's too baggy, but make sure that you have enough room on the side that you 'dress.'

**Cuffs:** They should hang straight all around, just brushing the top of the shoe. If the trousers have no cuffs, the hem should hang one-half to one inch longer in the back than it does in the front.

**Final Check:** Check that your trousers are comfortable — stoop, sit, and walk around a bit and see what they look like in the mirror.

### Skirts:

**Waist:** The waistband should fit snugly around your waist, with enough room for you to slide the flat of your hand between you and your skirt. Darts on either side of the waistband will emphasize your stomach, while gathers or pleats beneath the waistband will conceal it. Gathers at the back will hide a large behind.

**Hips:** There should be enough room for you to move your hips easily when walking or sitting down. Remember that the looser a skirt is over the hips the more you conceal — and vice versa.

**Length:** As hemlines rise and fall with each fashion season, there's no 'correct' length. As a general rule, tall women can wear skirts as long as they like, but smaller women should show more leg to create the illusion of greater height. Choose skirts not longer than about two inches below the knee if you are less than five feet four inches tall.

## Dresses

"No two garments are ever the same," says designer Bill Pashley, whose clients include the Princess of Wales and her two sisters, Lady Sarah McCorquodale and Lady Jane Fellowes. "If I cut two dresses from the same pattern, using identical fabric, they still turn out differently," he says. "One will go together like a dream and the other will fight me every inch of the way." He advises trying on at least two dresses of the same size when buying off the rack because the cut will always vary.

**Collars:** To give the illusion of a longer neckline, wear small or wide collars and keep them unbuttoned. Be careful when choosing a square neckline — they gape when they aren't properly cut. A T-shirt neck on a dress will make even a long neck look short. Heavy jowls can be softened with ruffles and wide bows.

*"Clothes don't fit now the way that they did before. When Dior was alive and those sort of couture houses were in full swing, a suit would literally stand up on its own. They were padded at the sides and hips, and some people called them 'suits of armour.' Today's looks are very soft and unstructured, but I should think that eventually the wheel will come full circle and we will be back in suits of armour."*
— Bill Pashley

**Shoulders:** There should be enough room for you to move your arms easily and comfortably raise them above your head. Unless the dress is worn off the shoulders or has drop shoulders, the shoulder seams should sit square on the shoulder line. If you are narrow shouldered you can put a pad under the shoulders for extra width. A gathered shoulder makes wide shoulders look smaller.

**Sleeves:** If the sleeves are too long, it looks as though you are waiting to grow into the dress. If they are too short, it looks as though you have grown out of it. Sleeves should reach to the wristbone.

*"All clothes that fit too tight look tarty. There should be room for you to move inside them without the clothes coming with you."*
— Bill Pashley

**Bodice:** Always try on dresses wearing the bra you intend to wear with that dress — a different bra may alter the position of the dress's bust darts and make them pucker. You can emphasize your bust by choosing a dress with a ruffled or gathered neckline that has a large bow. Anything fitted or clinging will draw attention to a large bust, as will solid colors, which have a more enlarging effect than prints and patterns.

**Length:** The hemline balances the design of a dress, so if you take it up or let it down, make sure you keep the proportions right.

## Slacks

**Men:** Flannels, tightly woven gabardines, and crisp cavalry twills should fit like suit trousers. Corduroys and casual trousers fit lower and closer to the hips.

**Women:** No amount of alterations will make your trousers fit if they're too tight when you buy them. They should have ample hip room and allow you to move with ease. The crotch should fit snugly without discomfort and without causing creases around the fly. Check that the side seams hang straight. If the trousers gape in the hips, waist or seat, they're too loose. If the waist has to be taken in more than an inch and a half, or if the fabric puckers under the waistband or behind, the trousers require major alterations. The cuffs should break over the front of the shoe and slope gently toward the back.

**Jeans:** Jean sizes vary with different manufacturers. They should never be so tight that it's a struggle to zip them up or uncomfortable to sit down in them. You should buy jeans that are a little on the long side because they tend to shrink a bit in the wash or during dry cleaning.

## Underwear

**Underwear/Men:** The three most popular styles of undershirt are the crew-neck T-shirt, the V-neck T-shirt and the sleeveless athletic shirt, which has a U-shaped neck opening. The crew neck and V-neck provide the most warmth, but the crew neck has the disadvantage of being visible under an open-necked shirt.

Undershirts are sized in inches according to chest measurement or as small, medium, large, and extra large. Because they now fit more closely to the body than they used to, they can be worn under tapered shirts without bunching or wrinkling.

Underpants are sized according to waist measurement. Boxer shorts, named after those the prize-fighters wear, are the most baggy. They tend to bunch up under jeans and tight fitting trousers. Briefs, with elastic waist and leg bands, fit more smoothly under tighter trousers. Bikinis are snug-fitting underpants modeled after European swimwear. They're usually made of light-weight nylon.

## Lingerie/Women

Thanks to the mini-skirt, women have never worn so little under their clothes as they do today. Garter belts, corsets, girdles and panty girdles were more or less abandoned in the '60s in favor of pantyhose and briefs. For many women, exercise classes now have to make up for that loss of support. As underwear has become less functional, it has also become more colorful, sexy, and fun.

However, nothing looks worse than underwear showing through your clothes. Flesh-colored lingerie is the most practical choice under a transparent blouse or dress, as long as your nipples don't show through your bra. A well-fitting bra should not pucker at the sides of the cups, and it should hold your breasts firm.

## Shirts and Sweaters

**Men's Shirts:** Men's shirts are sized by the circumference of the collar and the length of the sleeve measured from the nape of the neck to the base of the hand. The collar should fit close to the neck, but not so tight that it looks as though it is choking you, nor so loose that it gapes away from your neck. The number of buttons is important. There should be at least seven running down the front, with the last button well below the waistline to help keep the shirt tucked in .

**Women's Blouses:** A tailored blouse with one button open at the neck is suitable for business. Low necklines or frills down the front are best reserved for evening or social occasions. The shoulders should fit square and the sleeves should end where the hand joins the wrist.

**Sweaters:** Sweaters are sized by chest measurements or as small, medium, large, or extra large. The fit depends on the style. Close-fitting sweaters should fit snugly on the shoulders without being too tight under the arms. Sexy tight-fitting women's sweaters should outline the breasts without pulling across them. Today's fashionable loose-fitting sweaters always look baggy rather than stylish when they hang too far below the crotch or if the cuffs hang too loosely. Regardless of style, a sweater's cuffs should reach to the base of your hand or, in the case of turn-up cuffs, to the base of your thumb.

## Shoes

The average person walks the equivalent of two trips around the world in his lifetime, a fact that should be reason enough for buying shoes that fit.

**Socks/Pantyhose:** Wear socks that are as thick as the socks you'll be wearing with your new shoes. Women should put on their most textured hose, bearing in mind that shoes can be made smaller with a leather inner sole when thinner hose are worn.

**Sizing Up Your Shoes:** Notice the general feel of your shoes when you try them on. If they pinch at the heel or across the bridge of your foot, they are too tight. Toe room is critical to a comfortable fit. Your small toe shouldn't feel cramped and your big toe should be at least half an inch from the tip of your shoe. Allow yourself enough room to wiggle your toes easily. Your heel should feel snugly surrounded by the shoe, not as though the leather is cutting into it. But if your heel slips out of the shoe as you walk, the shoe is too big and will rub the back of your heel.

**Heels:** The weight of your body will force your foot deeper into high-heeled boots or shoes, so make sure as you walk that the shoes or boots are wide enough for comfort.

**Blazer:** The blazer was designed in 1850 by the captain of HMS Blazer, who wanted to smarten up the appearance of his crew. It became a favorite jacket of the yachting set and remains the most versatile jacket men or women can buy. Blazers come in different colors, but the traditional navy blue blazer with gold or silver buttons can be worn year-round if its fabric is a light wool or light wool-and-polyester mix.

Blazers have a tailored look and should fit like a suit jacket. Make sure the collar and lapels lie flat and that the jacket is roomy over the chest and hips. The shoulders should fit snugly but not so tight that you can't move your arms easily. Men's blazers are the same length as a suit jacket; women's blazers usually come to just below the hip.

**Men's Sports Jackets:** The fit of a sports jacket is similar to that of a blazer but it's cut about an inch longer. Norfolk tweed jackets, worn for shooting, are more generously cut to allow freedom of movement. These usually feature a yoke on the shoulder, a pleat down the middle of the back and a hint of a belt in the middle.

**Coats:** When choosing a coat, beware of horizontal or vertical wrinkles along its back, which indicate that the coat is too tight or too loose. Make sure the coat fits comfortably over your suits by wearing your heaviest suit when you try it on. The coat's sleeves should extend about half an inch beyond your shirt cuff.

**Length:** The length of a man's coat is more or less fixed at just below the knees, but a woman's coat should cover the skirt or dress underneath. As skirt and dress lengths vary with fashion, buying a coat is always a gamble, but it's safest to choose a coat on the longer side. Recent studies have shown that people perceive short coats as having less status and sex appeal than long ones, another reason for erring on the longer side.

**Tuxedo/Dinner Jacket:** First worn in England as a smoking jacket during the 1850s, when gentlemen retired to the smoking room for a cigar or cigarette after dinner so that the smell of tobacco wouldn't offend the ladies. The smoking jacket wasn't introduced to the United States until 1886 when a cosmopolitan young dandy wore it to the exclusive Tuxedo Park Ball in Tuxedo, New York. Since then, the tuxedo has gradually eclipsed the white tie and tails as formal wear. It is cut close to the body and its traditional color is black. It can be worn single or double breasted.

**Morning Coat:** Worn at weddings. It is a formal tailored garment cut to the contours of the body. The tails should end at the back of the knee, although the length can vary slightly to suit the physique.

*"With an evening coat and a white tie, anybody, even a stockbroker, can gain a reputation for being civilized."*

— Oscar Wilde,
*The Portrait of Dorian Gray*

# A GUIDE TO FABRICS

Nearly all fabrics come from fibers which have been spun into yarn and then woven or knitted into cloth of different weights and textures. After cloth has been created, it may be given a variety of 'finishes' — temporary or permanent — that help determine the characteristics of the garments made from it. Fabric making techniques and procedures are actually quite simple, and understanding them enables you to take better care of your clothes to make them look better and last longer.

## Fibers

There are both natural and man-made fibers. Natural fibers, such as cotton, linen, wool, and silk, are taken from natural animal or vegetable sources, while man-made fibers, such as rayon and nylon, are the result of chemical processing. Some man-made fibers are a combination of natural and synthetic products, while others are entirely synthesized. The fiber content of a fabric dictates its appearance, texture, and durability as well as most of its care and maintenance requirements.

Many fabrics are blends of different fibers. Although this may seem to complicate the problem of caring for a particular fabric, there is a general rule of thumb you should adopt. *Always treat blends as though the fabric is constructed of the most delicate fiber present.* For example, a shirt of a cotton and polyester blend should be pressed with a medium heat because, although cotton can tolerate a hot iron, polyester may melt. If you're not sure about the fiber content of a garment, check its care label. It will list the fibers present and provide instructions concerning the care and handling of the fabric.

## Finishes

Temporary finishes, which wear away after a few washings, are sometimes applied to poor quality fabrics to enhance their appearance. They include: *Sizing*, an application of wax, clay, or glue that can make a flimsy fabric appear heavier or stiffer. However, sizing will eventually wash out and although starch may restore some lost body, the garment will never be as crisp as it originally seemed.

Raw silk, which retains the natural resins the silk worm used to hold its cocoon together, is sometimes simulated by the process called *weighting*. This application of metallic salts may be used to restore body to silk that has had its resins removed, but weighting weakens fibers and causes the fabric to water spot very easily.

*Flocking* steams fibers into the back of wool fabrics to cover a loose weave. Clothing made from flocked fabric tends to wear out quickly.

## Permanent Finishes

Performance finishes are applied to fabrics to make them easier to care for. These finishes are usually listed on a garment's care label and include:

**Colorfast:** Fabrics will not bleed or fade if laundered according to directions.

**Crease Resistant:** The material has been treated to resist and recover from wrinkling caused by normal daily wear.

**Durable Press** or **Permanent Press:** Fabrics have been treated so that if they are removed from the dryer promptly they will require little or no ironing.

**Sanforized:** Fabric will not shrink more than one percent during laundering.

**Soil Release:** A treatment which makes it possible for permanent press fabrics to release oily stains.

**Stain** or **Spot Resistant:** Fabric has been treated to slow its normal absorption of oil-based materials. These fabrics resist stains — they aren't immune to them.

**Wash-and-Wear, Minimum Care** and **Easy Care:** These fabrics are constructed of fiber blends and require only machine washing and drying with little ironing or special attention.

# Fibers, Fabrics and Their Care

## Natural Fibers

### Cotton

**About the Fiber:** Cotton fabric is derived from the seed pods of the cotton plant. The fibers resemble ribbons of uniform thickness and vary in length from half an inch to two and one half inches. Naturally absorbent, cotton accepts dyes and finishes readily and can easily be spun into yarns of various weights and textures. Cotton is the most popular natural fiber and is often blended with man-made fibers to produce fabrics that are drip dry, wash-and-wear, or have other easy care qualities.

**Characteristics:** Cotton fabrics are strong (especially when wet), durable and static free. Cotton clothes are light-weight, cool, and comfortable. Unless cotton has been treated with a performance finish or combined with other fibers, it will wrinkle easily and may shrink during laundering. Cotton can be damaged by mildew and weakened by prolonged exposure to sunlight.

**Found In:** Cotton is present in just about every type of clothing imaginable, including garments made of broadcloth, corduroy, denim, gingham, organdy, piqué, poplin, seersucker, terrycloth, tweed, and velveteen.

**Care and Maintenance:** Because it is stronger when wet, cotton stands up well to machine washing. Adding a fabric softener to the rinse cycle will minimize cotton's natural wrinkling tendency.

As a rule, you should wash white cotton in hot water with a heavy duty detergent. Whites that seem a bit drab can be brightened with bleach or boiling, as long as you check the label first. Some finishes may react to chlorine, and fiber blends may be damaged by bleaches or extreme temperature. Colors should be washed separately in warm water.

Tumble dry at medium heat and remove clothing promptly to avoid scorching or setting wrinkles. 100% cotton fabrics should be pressed with a hot iron while they are still damp. Press until the fabric is dry. Again, refer to the care lable. *If the garment contains a fiber blend, set the iron for the most delicate fiber present.* Many man-made fibers will melt or sag when subjected to extreme heat. Iron on the wrong side of the material (except when setting creases or pleats) to minimize the polishing effect of heat and pressure.

### Linen

**About the Fiber:** Linen, a cellulose-based fiber that comes from the stalk of the flax plant, has been used since the beginning of recorded history and is noted for its strength, durability, and natural luster. The fibers are of random width and vary in length from five to twenty inches. Linen fabric, usually produced from a plain weave, can range from sheer to heavy.

**Characteristics:** Linen cloth is strong, durable, cool, comfortable, and highly absorbent. Dyed linen tends to bleed when washed and, like cotton, linen will shrink and wrinkle unless a performance finish has been applied. Linen does not produce lint and is not bothered by moths, but it may be damaged by mildew. Because the fiber is rather stiff, linen clothes have a tendency to wear out quickly at creases, edges, and folds.

**Found In:** Linen is a popular summer weight fabric and can be found in suits, blouses, shirts, dresses, slacks, and jackets.

**Care and Maintenance:** Linen suits should be dry cleaned to prevent shrinking and maintain their shape. Pre-shrunk linen can be washed with hot water and a heavy duty detergent. Dyed linen garments, and those that haven't been pre-shrunk, should be washed in warm water. Chlorine bleach will weaken linen, so use it only when absolutely necessary. Tumble dry at a medium heat and remove linen garments while very damp. If linen dries before it is pressed, the wrinkles will be very difficult to remove. Press on the wrong side with a hot iron after you've checked the care label to make sure that the fabric's finish can tolerate the heat. Instead of ironing in pleats and creases, use your fingers to shape the damp fabric. This will reduce the amount of wear and abrasion.

## Wool

**About the Fiber:** Wool is a protein-based fiber taken from the coats of goats and sheep. The fibers are generally between one and one half and 15 inches long and are crimped, which gives them a natural elasticity that makes them easy to spin into yarn. Each fiber is covered by tiny scales that lock together when subjected to heat and pressure and add to the strength, durability, and warmth of fabrics made from wool fibers.

**Characteristics:** Wool is pliable and holds its shape well, so it is easily tailored. It is highly absorbent and will hold quite a bit of water before feeling damp, yet its surface will tend to shed water. It holds dyes well and is naturally wrinkle resistant. Wool is, however, weak when wet and will stretch. It requires moth proofing, can be damaged by mildew and prolonged exposure to sunlight, and will shrink unless treated with a shrink-resistant finish.

**Found In:** Like cotton, wool is found in all types of clothing, from long underwear to top coats. It is typically used in fabrics such as flannel, crepe, tweed, jersey, serge, and gabardine.

**Care and Maintenance:** Wool is often ruined by improper handling, so always read a garment's care label before cleaning or trying to treat a stain. Don't over launder wool — a good brushing after it's worn will usually keep it fresh. Suits and coats should be dry cleaned while most other garments can be hand washed in cool water with a mild, soapless detergent. Never bleach wool — it will weaken the fiber and cause yellowing. When removing hand washed items from water, support the entire garment to keep it from stretching. Never machine dry wool. Instead, block the garment between towels on a flat surface away from artificial heat and direct sunlight. If the garment care label says the item is machine washable, use warm water and a mild detergent. Tumble dry at a low or moderate heat setting and remove the garment while slightly damp. If ironing is necessary, press it on the wrong side with a cloth and a cool iron. Wrinkles usually fall out of dry wool clothing if you hang it in the bathroom while you shower. If wool shrinks slightly, you may be able to reshape it after soaking it in a solution of mild hair shampoo and water. The shampoo will soften the fibers and allow you to gently stretch the garment back into shape.

## Silk

**About the Fiber:** Silk, a protein-based fiber, is taken from the cocoon of the silk worm. The cocoon is baked and then unraveled in a continuous filament that ranges from 1500 to 4000 feet in length. These filaments are then combined into fine threads which are strong, absorbent, resilient, and highly elastic.

**Characteristics:** Silk produces soft, glossy

material in many weights and weaves. Silk fabrics are warm, absorbent, and resistant to moths, mildew, and wrinkling. The term 'raw silk' refers to fabric which retains the natural adhesive resins that held the cocoon together. It has more body than fabric which has had these resins removed. Silk accepts dye quite readily but bright colors have a tendency to bleed when washed. Silk may yellow or fade from age, strong detergents, or a hot iron, and it can be weakened by exposure to sunlight and perspiration. Silk tends to build a static charge that causes garments to cling.

**Found In:** Silk is found in suits, dresses, blouses, garment linings, and lingerie. A versatile fiber, it is used in many materials, including brocade, chiffon, crepe, foulard, jersey, ninon, satin, taffeta, tweed, and velvet.

**Care and Maintenance:** Because silk garments are costly and fairly fragile, they are nearly always dry cleaned. If the care label specifies hand washing, use a mild detergent and tepid water. To dry, place the garment between two towels on a flat surface. Never use bleach or enzyme detergents on silk. If ironing is needed, use a cool iron over a cloth on the wrong side of the damp fabric.

# Man-made Fibers

## Acetate

**Trade Names:** *Acele, Avicolor, Avisco, Celanese, Celaperm, Celara, Chromspun, Estron.*

**About the Fiber:** Acetate is a cellulose-based, soft, silky-looking fiber that is often used in blends with silk, cotton, and rayon. It is relatively weak and tends to wrinkle and build a static charge.

**Characteristics:** Acetate can be dyed but is prone to fading. It is mildew and moth resistant, moderately absorbent and rarely stretches or shrinks. Acetate is weakened by light, softened by hot water, and can be damaged by mild acids and acetone solvents.

**Found In:** Acetate is frequently used in blends. It is found in brocade, crepe, faille, jersey, lace, taffeta, and tricot. It is also blended with wool to produce hand knitting yarns.

**Care and Maintenance:** Acetate should be dry cleaned unless the garment care label says otherwise. If the fabric is washable, use warm water and a mild detergent. Tumble dry briefly on a moderate heat setting, or drip dry away from artificial heat sources. Hand washing in a mild detergent solution and then letting the fabric drip dry is preferable. Acetate can sag or melt at high temperatures, so use a cool iron over a cloth on the wrong side of the fabric to press it. When treating spots or stains never use acetone or nail polish, which will damage the fabric — use pure amyl acetate instead.

## Acrylic

**Trade Names:** *Acrilan, Creslan, Courtelle, Orlon, Zefkrome, Zefran.*

**About the Fiber:** Acrylic is a soft, strong, light-weight fiber that accepts dyes well and remains colorfast. It is not very absorbent and will dry quickly.

**Characteristics:** Acrylic is produced in a variety of weights and textures. Textured acrylic yarns feel and wear much like wool. Fabrics tend to be wrinkle resistant and hold creases and pleats well. They also have excellent resistance to moths, mildew, and chemicals. Although they won't fade from direct sunlight, acrylic fabrics are heat sensitive and may melt or sag when dried or ironed.

**Found In:** Acrylic gives easy care qualities to blended fabrics. It's found in knitting yarns, sweaters, dress fabrics, athletic wear and strong work clothes.

**Care and Maintenance:** Acrylic fabrics may be dry cleaned or machine washed. To launder at home, treat spots and stains before washing to avoid setting them permanently. A fabric softener will minimize acrylic's tendency to build a static charge. Chlorine bleach is generally safe for acrylic whites, but check the care label to be sure. Tumble dry on low heat and remove promptly. Ironing usually isn't necessary, but if you want to press acrylic use a cool iron on the wrong side of the fabric. Washing in hot water or pressing with a hot iron will soften the fiber and cause the fabric to sag and wrinkle permanently.

## Nylon

**Trade Names:** *Antron, Blue C, Caprolan, Cedilla, Celanese, Enkalure, Monvelle, Quiana, Touch, Ultron.*

**About the Fiber:** Nylon is an extremely strong, elastic fiber that holds dyes, resists wrinkles, and is not particularly absorbent.

**Characteristics:** Nylon fabrics hold pleats and creases well. They are generally easy to maintain, highly resistant to moths and mildew, and will not soil easily. Nylon fabrics tend to retain body heat.

**Found In:** Nylon is often used in stockings, lingerie, dress fabrics, suit fabrics, stretch material, and sports wear.

**Care and Maintenance:** White nylon fabrics should be washed in warm water with a heavy duty detergent; colors require cool water. Wash whites separately to keep them from picking up traces of dye and turning gray. If this does happen, or if a yellow tinge develops, use peroxygen bleach such as sodium perborate. Never use chlorine bleach, which can severely damage nylon. Adding fabric softener during laundering will help reduce static cling, and a cold rinse will usually remove any wrinkles. Tumble dry on low heat, or drip dry. Nylon usually doesn't require ironing, but if it is necessary you can press the fabric on the wrong side while it's still damp. Use a cool iron.

## Polyester

**Trade Names:** *Avlin, Blue C, Dacron, Encron, Fortrel, Kodel, Quintess, Trevira, Vycron.*

**About the Fiber:** Polyester is available in a variety of textures and weights and is often blended with other fabrics to give them its easy care traits. It is durable, wrinkle-resistant, and retains pleats and creases well.

**Characteristics:** Fabrics containing polyester tend to hold body heat. They are resistant to moths and mildew, and are noted for their low absorbency. They are, however, susceptible to yellowing and can be damaged by heat. Polyester is blended with cotton to create fabrics that are drip dry and permanent press, and with wool to create suit fabrics that are durable and have smooth finishes.

**Found In:** Polyester is blended with natural and man-made fibers to produce woven and knitted fabrics. It is often found in slacks, skirts, shirts, blouses, lingerie, and suits.

**Care and Maintenance:** Tailored polyester fabrics should be dry cleaned when needed. Otherwise, machine wash sturdy white or light colored polyester with warm water and a heavy duty detergent. Launder bright colors separately in cool water. Chlorine bleach is usually safe for use on whites, but always check the garment care label before you use it. Adding a fabric softener to the cycle will reduce static build up. Avoid hot water, which can damage the fibers. Tumble dry using a low to moderate heat setting and remove promptly at the end of the cycle to avoid scorching and wrinkling. If ironing is necessary, use a moderate temperature and press after the garment has dried.

## Rayon

**Trade Names:** *Avicolor, Avril, Bemberg, Coloray, Cupioni, Englo, Enka, Enkrome, Zantrel.*

**About the Fiber:** Rayon is a relatively weak, man-made, cellulose-based fiber which can be manufactured to resemble natural fibers in light or heavy weights, with napped or smooth textures. It takes dye well and is generally colorfast.

**Characteristics:** Rayon produces soft, comfortable, absorbent fabrics. Unless treated with a performance finish, rayon will wrinkle easily and shrink when laundered. It is susceptible to mildew and can be weakened by prolonged exposure to sunlight.

**Found In:** Highly versatile, rayon is found in dresses, suits, blouses, coats, lingerie, and slacks.

**Care and Maintenance:** Because they tend to stretch and shrink when washed, most rayon garments are dry cleaned. If the label says the garment is washable, use warm water and a mild detergent. Support the entire garment when lifting it from the water and place it flat on a towel to dry. Chlorine or a peroxygen bleach such as sodium perborate can usually be used on whites but check the label first. Don't dry rayon fabrics in direct sunlight. Iron with a medium heat while the fabric is still damp, preferably on the wrong side of the garment.

## Spandex

**Trade Name:** *Arnel.*

**About the Fiber:** Triacetate is a man-made cellulose-based fiber with relatively little strength. It takes dye easily, is generally colorfast, and is used frequently in fiber blends. Triacetate is similar to acetate but is more resistant to heat.

**Found In:** Triacetate is usually blended with other fibers and is found in fabrics such as tricot, sharkskin, flannel, taffeta, and jersey.

**Care and Maintenance:** Triacetate stands up well to machine washing and drying. Pleated garments should be hand washed and placed on a hanger to dry, while other clothing can be tumble dried using medium heat. Remove promptly to minimize wrinkling, although triacetate blends usually require some ironing. Iron these fabrics on the wrong side while still damp. *Note:* When treating stains on triacetate fabrics never use acetone or any other organic solvent as these can severely damage the fibers.

The following list will give you an idea of the variety of fabrics available, the fibers most often used in their construction, and some general rules for their care.

# Fabric Glossary

**Batiste** is a light-weight, soft, smooth, plain-weave fabric. It is usually made from cotton, but it can also be linen, silk, or rayon. Batiste is white or pastel and can be found in handkerchiefs, lingerie, blouses, soft dresses, and children's wear. Handle this material according to the fiber content listed on the label.

**Bedford Cloth** is a strong, durable, ribbed fabric of wool, silk, cotton, synthetic, or blended fibers. Characterized by a distinct rounded rib that runs the length of the fabric, it is used in dresses, suits, coats, trousers, sports wear, and children's clothing. Wool bedford cloth should be dry cleaned; other varieties should be treated according to the garment care instructions on the label.

**Bouclé** is a woven or knitted fabric distinguished by looped or knotted yarns. It is usually made from wool but it occasionally includes blended cotton or man-made fibers. It is used primarily in dresses and coats and should be dry cleaned unless the care label recommends otherwise.

**Broadcloth** is a tightly woven fabric with fine ribs running across the surface. It is found in a variety of weights, fibers, and blends, and is used for many types of clothing. Cotton and cotton blends are favorites for shirts and blouses. Launder according to the fiber content of the fabric.

**Calico** is a light-weight, unfinished, plain-weave cotton fabric that usually has a small print and a slightly rough texture. Handle it as you would cotton unless the fabric is a fiber blend, which should be laundered according to the needs of its weakest fiber.

**Cambric** is an inexpensive, fine, plain-weave cotton or linen fabric. While usually white, cambric may be found in solid colors. Launder according to the fiber content. Light starch will restore the somewhat stiff appearance of this fabric.

**Challis** is an expensive, delicate, very soft, plain-weave woolen with a faint ribbed texture. You'll find it in ties, shirts, and sweaters. Challis should be hand washed.

**Chiffon** is a delicate, soft, plain-weave fabric of silk or occasionally rayon. Most chiffon should be dry cleaned. However, if the label specifies hand washing, handle it as you would silk. Press chiffon with a cool iron, reshaping the garment as you work.

**Corduroy** is a cotton or cotton blend fabric in plain or twill-weave. This strong fabric has distinct cords that run along its length. It is found in slacks, jackets, and heavy shirts. It is best to hand wash corduroy, although most garments can be machine washed as well. Before you iron corduroy, while the fabric is slightly damp, smooth the cord in the direction of the nap with a cloth. Press with a warm iron on the wrong side of the fabric. If the garment has a lining, it should be dry cleaned instead.

**Crepe** has a rough, puckered surface that is achieved through embossing, weaving, chemical processing, or the use of highly twisted yarns. It may be silk, cotton, wool, synthetic, or a fiber blend. Handle crepe according to the fibers listed on the label.

**Denim** is made of a twill-weave fabric of cotton or a cotton blend. The weave is characterized by solid color threads running across the fabric and white threads running its length. It is found in jeans, suits, skirts, jackets, and heavy shirts. Denim, which tends to shrink and bleed, should be laundered according to the instructions on the care label.

**Drill** is a durable, medium-weight, double-weave fabric of cotton or blended cotton. Drill is easily laundered — just handle it as you would cotton or, in the case of blends, treat it as you would its weakest fiber.

**Felt** is one of the few fabrics that is neither woven nor knitted. Instead, felt is produced by subjecting a mat of fibers to heat and moisture while under pressure. It is usually wool, fur, or mohair but it can contain cotton or rayon fibers. Felt shrinks easily and should be dry cleaned.

**Flannel** is a soft cotton or wool fabric with a plain or twill-weave. It frequently has a short nap covering the weave and is used in heavy shirts, suits, jackets, and coats. Flannel clothing should be laundered like wool or dry cleaned.

**Gabardine** is a very tight twill-weave fabric made of cotton or wool. It may occasionally contain blends of polyester or rayon. Gabardine is durable and tailors well, so it is often found in suits, coats, trousers and, when treated with resins, rainwear. Brush gabardine after wearing and dry clean periodically.

**Georgette** is a sheer, luxurious fabric of silk, wool, or synthetic fibers. Its textured surface is similar to crepe and its weight is slightly heavier than chiffon. Because it is delicate, georgette should be dry cleaned. If the care label specifically recommends hand washing, then treat it as you would silk.

**Grosgrain** is a firm, close-weave fabric with a silky appearance and a small but pronounced rib running across the face of the fabric. It is made from silk or synthetic fibers and should be dry cleaned.

**Harris Tweed** is a trade name for woolen fabric that is dyed, spun, and hand woven on Harris or one of the other islands of the Outer Hebrides off the coast of northern Scotland. It is found in suits, jackets, and topcoats. Tweed should be brushed firmly after wear and dry cleaned when necessary.

**Hopsacking** is a plain or basket-weave fabric of cotton, linen, or rayon. It has a rough surface and is usually found in jackets or slacks. Launder according to the fiber content of the fabric.

**Jersey** is a soft knit fabric which originated on the Isle of Jersey and is available in weights that range from sheer to heavy. It may be made of cotton, wool, silk, acrylic, polyester, and rayon. Jersey is used to make lingerie, sweaters, shirts, and coats. Wool and rayon jersey should be dry cleaned. All other fibers should be handled according to the garment care label instructions.

**Lace** is an open work fabric of cotton, rayon, or nylon with finely detailed patterns of looped, knotted or twisted threads. It is used principally in the trimming of blouses and dresses. Lace used to be hand-made, although today most of it is produced by machine. It is best to hand wash lace according to its fiber content. Press with low to moderate heat while the lace is covered with a slightly damp cloth. Work slowly and reshape it as you go. Antique lace should be dry cleaned.

**Lamé** is a fabric of man-made metallic threads. It is sometimes combined with silk or synthetic fibers and is most often used in evening wear. Dry clean lamé unless the care label instructs otherwise.

**Lawn**, a sheer fabric of carded cotton or linen, has a crisp appearance. It is produced in white, colors, and prints and may be found in light-weight garments such as blouses and summer dresses. Handle lawn as you would cotton.

**Moiré** is an irregular wavy horizontally patterned finish found on corded or ribbed fabric. It is made of silk, cotton, or synthetic fibers. The patterned finish is the result of engraved rollers used during the finishing process. Dry clean moiré, as its surface can be damaged by water.

**Muslin** is a term used to describe a variety of plain-weave cotton fabrics with textures that range from sheer to coarse. These fabrics may be bleached, unbleached, colored, or printed, and can be found in underwear, shirts, blouses, skirts and dresses. Muslin should be hand washed in warm water with a mild detergent. Lay the garment on a towel and reshape to dry. Press while still damp on the wrong side of the fabric.

**Organdy** is an extremely fine cotton fabric made with tightly twisted yarns that give it a crisp finish. It is found primarily in blouses and should be laundered according to the label's instructions.

**Oxford Cloth** is a popular cotton fabric produced by using two fine warp or crossing yarns with a heavier filling yarn to yield a firm yet soft and lustrous finish. Oxford cloth is usually found in shirts and should be laundered like cotton or according to the care label instructions if the fabric is a blend.

**Piqué** is a strong cotton or synthetic fiber material which has cords or welts running the length of the fabric. It can be a plain-weave fabric or have a pattern woven into or embossed upon its surface. Launder piqué according to its fiber content. To avoid crushing the pile, iron it over a cloth on the wrong side of the fabric.

**Poplin** is a smooth, firm plain-weave fabric with a fine rib running across its surface. It is usually cotton, although synthetics are becoming more common. It is similar to cotton broadcloth but has a slightly larger rib. Poplin is used in suits, jackets, blouses, top coats and when waterproofed, rainwear. Suits and rainwear should be dry cleaned; other items should be laundered according to the fibers they contain.

**Satin** is a luxurious fabric of silk or synthetic fibers made from a satin-weave. It is available in a variety of weights ranging from sheer crepe satin to relatively stiff duchess satin. It is used extensively in lingerie and dresses. Dry clean or follow the instructions on the care label when laundering. If pressing is necessary, use a cool iron on the wrong side of the fabric.

**Seersucker** is a light-weight, plain-weave, cotton or cotton blend fabric with an irregular puckered surface that results from alternating the tension of yarns during the weaving process. Seersucker is found in suits, jackets, slacks and skirts and should be dry cleaned or laundered according to the garment care label instructions.

**Serge** is a crisp, flat twill or plain-weave fabric available in a variety of weights. Traditionally a wool fabric, serge is now made with cotton and blended fibers for longer life. This durable, easily tailored fabric is often used in men's suits. Brush apparel after wearing and periodically dry clean.

**Shantung** was originally made of wild silk whose irregular strands produced an uneven effect in the weave. Today synthetics are used to duplicate this characteristic. Shantung can be found in suits, jackets, dresses and ties. Dry clean or launder according to the care label instructions. When ironing is needed, press with a cool iron on the wrong side of the fabric after it has dried.

**Sharkskin** is twill-weave wool fabric which is produced by alternating a white yarn with another color, usually black, brown, or blue, in the weave. It can be found in suits and topcoats. Brush after wearing to remove dust and freshen the garment's appearance. Dry clean when needed.

**Taffeta** refers to a group of fine, slightly stiff,

plain-weave fabrics which are lustrous. Originally produced from silk, most taffeta is now made from synthetic fibers. Silk taffeta should be dry cleaned. Synthetics can be hand washed gently using warm water and a mild detergent. Rinse thoroughly with cool water and drip dry. If any ironing is required, use a low setting on the wrong side of the slightly damp fabric.

**Tweed** is a woven, rough-surfaced, woolen fabric which employs fiber dying to create its distinctive coloring. It is used in suits, jackets, trousers, skirts and top coats. Tweed should be brushed firmly after being worn. When cleaning is required, dry clean.

**Velour** is a soft, smooth, close-weave fabric with a short pile brushed in one direction to produce a velvet-like feel. It is made from a variety of man-made and natural fibers and may be found in dressing gowns, suits, dresses, and coats. Wool velour should be dry cleaned when necessary; for other types of velour, check the garment care label for handling instructions.

**Velvet** is an expensive fabric with a short, dense pile and a luxurious finish. Originally made only of silk, it is now available in a variety of fibers. Silk velvet and cotton velvet should be dry cleaned. Refer to the garment care label for instructions concerning the handling of other fibers. To remove wrinkles and creases, you can press velvet with several towels covering the fabric to protect the pile, although it's a better idea to hang the garment in the bathroom while you shower and let the steam remove the wrinkles.

**Velveteen** is a less expensive cotton fabric with a short, tight pile designed to resemble velvet. Handle it as you would velvet.

**Voile** is a light-weight, sheer, plain-weave fabric composed of tightly twisted yarns that produce a crisp feel. It is similar to lawn and organdy but not quite as stiff. Voile can be made with a variety of natural or man-made fibers, so check the garment care label for handling instructions before laundering. When drying, place the garment between towels and lay on a flat surface. Press voile while it is still damp. Reshape it as you work.

*"I don't think that color has anything to do with making you look older or younger, except when you wear a color that cheers you up you tend to look younger because you look happier."*

— Bill Pashley

# BRUSHING

Brushing is an essential part of clothes care. It freshens clothes and saves on wear and tear by removing abrasive dust. Heavy-weight clothes and wool suits need the most vigorous brushing, and if you brush them before pressing you will be able to remove the unwanted creases more easily.

Proper brushing techniques were one of the first things any footman or housemaid learned about caring for clothes. Grand houses had special brushing rooms set aside where footmen brushed their employers' clothes and looked after guests' clothes when they came to stay for weekends, the busiest time of the week. Everything needed to look after clothes was in the brushing room — and not much else. There was usually a long work table in the middle of the room, a couple of sinks, and some tall cupboards lining the walls for storing the cleaning equipment. The valet usually had his own brushing room — he comandeered an empty room and adapted it to suit his preferences. A lady's maid cleaned and pressed her lady's clothes in her own room, and the housemaids used the housemaids' room which also served as the housemaids' sitting room.

# Clothes Brushes

Natural bristles are better than synthetic ones, which are stiffer and may scratch the material. A good natural bristle clothes brush, like the ones made by *Kent of London*, is expensive but you'll never need to replace it. It will last you a lifetime.

There is a wide variety of clothes brush styles to choose from. A dandy brush, the brush used for grooming horses, can be used on tough fabrics. Use a special wire brush for suede garments. A velvet-faced lint brush, excellent for evening clothes and finely woven soft fabrics, is the most effective tool for picking up lint and hairs. Removing these bits and pieces with your fingernails takes time, and removing them with sticky tape wound around your hand (adhesive side out) sometimes leaves a mark.

# How to Brush

It's easiest to brush clothes on a sturdy wooden table. If the table's surface is highly polished, cover it with a blanket to protect the shine and then cover the blanket with a sheet to prevent fluff from getting on your clothes. Or, if you prefer, you can hang your clothes on a door frame so that they are within easy reach and you can brush around them.

Brushing requires a strong sweeping motion or a firm flick of your wrist in places where dust gathers. Never use a scrubbing motion. This only wears the material and rubs in dust and dirt, obviously the last thing you want to do. Brush out marks with short quick strokes, and don't jab at the cloth — you might tear it. Brush up the nap — i.e. against the natural grain of the material — to remove the dust, then brush downward for a smooth finish.

Use a damp brush to freshen up winter clothes. Dip the bristles of your brush into a bowl of water with a couple of drops of ammonia added for a softening effect. Flick the water from the bristles of your brush so that it's slightly damp, not wet. As you brush, look for stains and remove them as you go along.

## Fabrics

**Wool:** Brush briskly up and down the nap to get rid of dust on heavy suitings. You can use a dandy brush on stout tweeds and heavy overcoats, but camel's hair and lighter woolens should be brushed more gently with a natural bristle clothes brush. Closely woven twills and synthetics don't need much brushing because dust doesn't stick to them.

**Velvet:** Always work down the nap, because brushing upward will leave a mark. Use a brush faced with velvet to pick up fluff and hairs. Failing that, gently rub a piece of velvet down the nap of the garment. Never use a bristle brush on velvet — it will damage the fabric.

**Silk:** Silk dresses and silk robes pick up fluff that can be removed with a slightly damp tea towel. It is important that the tea towel be only just damp — if it's too wet the material will crease.

**Fur:** Fur gathers about 10 times as much dust as other garments, but combing or brushing can damage the hairs. Instead, give it a shake after each wearing, and remember to shake it every now and again if you have not worn it for a while.

*"Dust makes suits grimy. Brushing removes dust, and the need for dry cleaning. I think frequent dry cleaning is a waste of money and shortens the life of a suit. By brushing a suit after it has been worn and by cleaning stains as they appear, you eliminate the need for dry cleaning. You should only need to take a suit to the cleaners three or four times in its lifetime. If you are cleaning your suit once a month, you're knocking years off it."*

— Mark Fairweather

**Linen, Cotton and Synthetic Fibers:** These need brushing after every three or four wearings. Lighter colors need even less, because they show dirt more and need to be washed or dry cleaned instead.

## Suits

Wool and heavy-weight suits need brushing after each wearing — at the very least give them a shake before you put them away. A suit you haven't worn for a while will quite often need brushing to freshen it before you put it on.

"It takes time to learn how to brush and press clothes properly, but once you know how it's amazingly easy," observes Mark Fairweather, who has been in service since 1974 and is First Footman to England's royal family.

One of his duties is acting as valet to the Queen's guests, who have included virtually all the crowned heads of Europe. He says, "It takes me only two minutes to brush a suit properly and five minutes to press it. In the morning I turn on the iron before I go up to the guest's bedroom to collect his suit, so that when I come back to the footmen's room the iron is hot enough to start pressing. I brush the suit before I press it, then I press it and return it to his wardrobe — all in about 10 minutes." The following methods of brushing a jacket, waistcoat and trousers are those used by Mark Fairweather.

**Waistcoat:** Because it's worn underneath your jacket, it won't collect much dust. Just lay it lining side down with the buttons undone and brush up and down the nap to and from the shoulders.

## How Mark Fairweather Brushes a Jacket

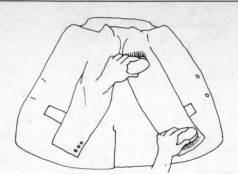

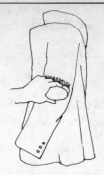

**1.** Undo the buttons and empty the pockets.

**2.** Start on the collar. Hold the jacket so that the lining faces you. Turn out the collar to brush the interfacing. Hold it in your left hand with your thumb on top and your fingers curled underneath to support it. Slide the collar through your left hand as you brush across it with your right hand. Turn the collar over to brush the right side with short brisk strokes.

**3.** Brush the shoulders. The jacket lining should face you. Put your left hand inside the first shoulder with your palm facing downward so that the shoulder lies on the back of your hand. For extra support, spread out your fingers and slightly curl them to the shape of the shoulder.

**4.** Use your right hand to brush down the nap from the

inside edge of the collar to the outside edge of the shoulder until all traces of dust and dandruff have disappeared.

**5.** Next, as long as your jacket is reasonably clean, you can brush the front of the first sleeve from the shoulder to the cuff. However, if it looks drab or has not been brushed for a while, brush the second shoulder and leave the sleeves alone until you reach step 7.

**6.** Brush the second shoulder. If the jacket is clean, continue brushing the sleeves as described in step 3. If not, follow steps 7 and 8.

**7.** In order to get the front of the sleeves really clean, lay the jacket flat with the lining side face down on a sturdy table top. Fold the sleeves back and brush up the nap from the cuff to the shoulder and down the nap from the shoulder to the cuff.

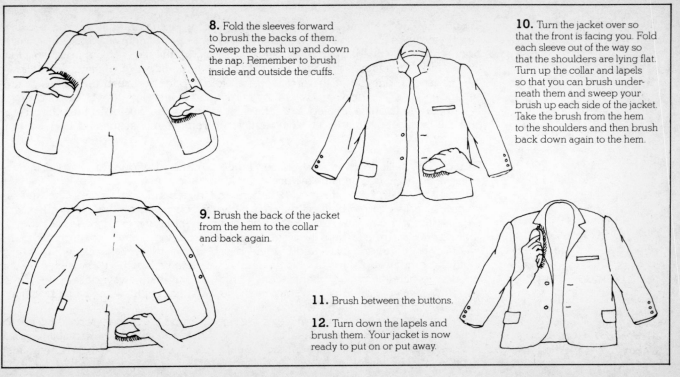

**8.** Fold the sleeves forward to brush the backs of them. Sweep the brush up and down the nap. Remember to brush inside and outside the cuffs.

**9.** Brush the back of the jacket from the hem to the collar and back again.

**10.** Turn the jacket over so that the front is facing you. Fold each sleeve out of the way so that the shoulders are lying flat. Turn up the collar and lapels so that you can brush underneath them and sweep your brush up each side of the jacket. Take the brush from the hem to the shoulders and then brush back down again to the hem.

**11.** Brush between the buttons.

**12.** Turn down the lapels and brush them. Your jacket is now ready to put on or put away.

**Trousers:** Lay the trousers flat with one leg on top of the other. If they have cuffs, turn them down to brush out the dust that gets kicked into them as you walk. Always brush trousers with long sweeping strokes. Brush up the nap — from the cuff to the waistband — to uncover the dust, and then smooth the nap by brushing downward.

Brush the outside of the first leg, then fold it back to brush the inside of the second leg. As you brush, look out for marks and stains. Turn the trousers over to brush the inside of the first leg. Pull it back, then brush the outside of the second leg and the fly. Use a commercial stain remover to remove any stains and to get rid of the odor.

**Skirts:** The skills Mademoiselle Elise Gaubert learned for looking after skirts and dresses come from a lifetime's work in looking after women's clothes. In 1922 she arrived in England from France to become a lady's maid. "At a time," she recalls, "when all ladies had to be foreign, preferably French." Among the many ladies she worked for were Nancy Astor (when her permanent lady's maid Rose was away), and Elizabeth Arden when she visited England. "Ladies' clothes need gentle treatment," Mlle. Gaubert says, "and I would brush them far less vigorously than men's clothes. Some tweed skirts are too soft and delicate to be brushed, in which case it's enough to give them a good shake each time you put them away. But whatever the material, always brush down the nap from the waistband to the hem; if you brush up the nap, you might loosen the threads."

"Lay the skirt face down on a firm surface. Start on the back, saving the front to last as it shows the most. When brushing a pleated skirt use the corner of your clothes brush to brush between each pleat — you'd be surprised how much dust accumulates in the folds."

*"Brush inside the pleats of a pleated skirt, because dust gathers there."*
— Mlle. Odile Barbiere

## Dresses, Jeans and Sweaters

Mlle. Gaubert recalls: "I brushed my lady's clothes every time she wore them. I used to brush her clothes straight after she took them off. She might change three or four times during the day, and it was part of my job to help her. The people I worked for had the most beautiful clothes made by Worth, Poiret, Chanel or any of the top couturiers in Paris. The way I looked after their clothes is the way that I still look after mine. I always brush my skirts and dresses before I put them away, and I make sure that there are no loose threads or buttons, and that the hem isn't falling down. I shake sweaters after each wearing to get rid of the hairs, dandruff and little bits of fluff. I brush them whenever they need it, and always after three or four wearings."

## How Mlle. Elise Gaubert Brushes a Dress

Brush the collar, shoulders and sleeves of a dress the same way you brush them on a jacket, but because the material is more delicate, brush more gently with lighter strokes. Start with the collar — hold it in your left hand and brush each side of it with your right hand. Use short brisk strokes and work across it. Support the first shoulder with one hand and brush it with the other hand. Then brush the sleeve from the shoulder to the cuff. Brush the second shoulder and sleeve before starting on the rest of the dress. Lay the dress face down on a covered table and brush the back of the sleeves, including inside and outside the cuffs as these tend to get grimy. Fold the arms out of the way before starting on the back. Always work on the bodice before the skirt so that any dust that falls on the skirt can be brushed off later. Brush downward from the collar to the waist and then from the waist to the hem.

Turn the dress over and brush the front the same way you brushed the back, using long sweeping strokes.

**Jeans:** "Brushing softens jeans — it takes the stiffness out of new jeans that haven't been prewashed, and out of jeans that have been machine or hand washed," says Frank Hurd, who has been in service for many years. "I dress up when I serve a formal dinner," he says, "but as soon as I've finished I get back into a pair of jeans. I live in jeans. I must have at least 30 or 40 pairs and a good many are over five or six years old, but I can still wear them because I've bothered to look after them."

**Sweaters:** It always pays to brush acrylic, lambswool and cashmere after each wearing, but you should never brush shetland wool, angora or mohair as the bristles can tear these more fragile wools. All sweaters benefit from a good airing, especially if they have been worn in a smoky atmosphere.

The softer a brush, the better it is for brushing wool. Use a soft natural bristle clothes brush or even a child's hairbrush. Lay the sweater face down on a sturdy table top. Brush across the back from shoulder to shoulder. Brush the sleeves from the tip of the shoulder to the ends of the cuffs (as shown). Brush inside and outside the cuffs before starting on the rest of the back. Use light, even strokes to brush from the collar to the hem. Brush the front the same way. Remove marks with a damp Irish linen tea towel or an old damask napkin as these won't leave lint behind.

Use a *D-Fuzz-It* sweater and fabric comb to get rid of fuzz on lambswool, cashmere, and acrylic sweaters. (It also works on woven or knitted fabrics, coats and blankets.) Hold the sweater taut with one hand and use the other to brush downward.

## Hats and Coats

### Hats:

There was a time when no man was properly dressed for the office unless he turned up wearing a hat, and a woman felt undressed if she went out without one. Over the past few decades women's hats have gradually lost out to hairstyles and men's hats are seen less frequently as business wear becomes less formal. But the best way to keep them clean hasn't changed.

**2.** Start brushing in a clockwise direction. Work above the ribbon and continue upward to the top of the crown. As you brush, turn the hat by rotating your left wrist counterclockwise.

**3.** When you have finished the crown, brush around the brim in exactly the same way.

### Felt Hats and Bowlers:

Brush them after each wearing near a boiling kettle to let the steam bring up the nap.

**1.** Place the upturned palm of your left hand inside the crown. Press your thumb against the headband on one side and spread your fingers to balance the inside crown.

### Riding Hats:

Use a soft natural bristle clothes brush and work near a boiling kettle to raise the nap. Hold it as you would a bowler or felt hat and smooth the nap by rotating your left wrist counterclockwise and brushing the hat in the same direction with your right hand.

## Coats:

Because a coat is heavier and bulkier than a jacket you must arrange it differently to brush it.

**1.** Make sure the pockets are empty and undo the buttons.

**2.** Hold the coat in one hand with the lining facing you. Use your free hand to start brushing the wrong side (the interfacing), then turn the collar over to brush the right side.

**3.** Hang the coat on a door frame or low picture hook with the back facing you.

**4.** Brush from the inside edge of the collar to the outside edge of each shoulder.

**5.** Hold the first sleeve taut with your free hand, and with your other hand brush from the cuff to the shoulder and back again.

**6.** Brush the back of the second sleeve the same way.

**10.** To brush the front of the coat, turn the collar and lapels up and brush underneath them. Then hold the hem taut and brush up and down the nap. Finish by brushing between the buttons. Turn the collar and lapels down and give them a final brush.

**7.** Hold the hem taut with one hand. With the other hand, sweep the brush up and down the back.

**8.** Turn the coat around so that the front is facing you.

**9.** Brush the front of the sleeves the same way that you brushed the back. Brush inside and outside the cuffs.

# FOLDING AND STORING CLOTHES

Leaving clothes lying about on a chair or on the floor not only looks messy, it also wrinkles them and can add lumps and bumps in the wrong places. It doesn't take long to put clothes away properly, and careful storage can make a huge difference in what your clothes look like and how long they last.

Hanging clothes up when they're warm from the heat of your body allows the creases to fall out, but don't put them back in the closet the minute you take them off. Put them on a hanger and give them a good airing first to get rid of the stale odors. Always empty your pockets before hanging clothes, because loose change and keys can stretch and wear fabric. And take out all pens or pencils — many a favorite suit has been ruined by a leaky pen. Brush your clothes to get rid of lint or dust and check for any tears or missing buttons that should be repaired before they're put away. Sort out garments that should be washed or dry cleaned and put these in a separate pile for laundering. Clothes deserve as much rest as you do, so don't wear the same thing two days running. Give it a chance to recover, to stay looking its best.

# How to Arrange Your Closet

A tidy closet saves time by allowing you to grab exactly what you want without having to search through endless items of clothing to find it. "Hang your clothes so that they all face the same way," recommends footman Mark Fairweather, who keeps wardrobes at Buckingham Palace in shipshape order. "Subdivide each group into business and informal wear," he explains, "then have all your light-weight suits next to each other, followed by jackets, skirts, dresses, and trousers. Do the same with your medium-weight clothes and your winter wardrobe." He suggests that you keep winter coats, jeans and formal evening clothes away from the rest of your wardrobe. "Coats can push up against other clothes and crush them," he explains. "I like to hang the evening clothes where I can easily keep an eye on them to see that they are in good repair. And since jeans are worn year-round, it's easiest to keep them in their own section instead of categorizing them by season or fabric weight."

Veteran lady's maid Mademoiselle Elise Gaubert once looked after a woman who had enough closet space to leave six inches between each garment. Nothing was ever crushed, she recalls, and the clothes had room to breathe, which reduced the need for pressing, ironing, and cleaning. Most of us don't have that amount of space, but your closet should be deep enough to accommodate the width of your clothes without pushing the shoulders against the wall or closet door.

Make sure your clothes aren't jammed up against each other — there should be enough space to allow air to circulate around them. If your closet is small, make more room by storing out-of-season clothes somewhere other than the closet that you use every day. Twice a year, get rid of all the clutter that isn't worth keeping in your closet. Be ruthless. Sell or give away anything you haven't worn in over a year—even that expensive mistake in mint condition.

**Hangers:** Use wooden, plastic, or padded hangers—never the wire hangers you get from the cleaners. These are flimsy, prone to rust that can rub off on your clothes, and so thin that they sometimes leave a ridge in the shoulders. Double-barred wooden hangers are best for men's suits because they are strong enough to take the weight of a three-piece suit. You can fold the trousers over the lower bar and arrange the waistcoat and jacket on the top bar so that they won't get separated in the closet. Plastic or wooden wishbone hangers, gently curved to match the contours of your shoulders and back, are ideal for coats and jackets. Soft padded hangers work well for dresses and long cardigans because they are less likely to stretch delicate fabrics out of shape.

Whatever hanger you choose, make sure it doesn't extend beyond the line of the shoulder or it will poke into the sleeve and leave a mark. Clamp hangers, or hangers with clips, are useful for hanging skirts. Because clamp hangers clip over the waistband, the skirt hangs straighter and is less likely to stretch to an uneven length than when it is hung from the fabric loops found inside the waistband. You can hang trousers over a double-barred hanger or use a springloaded trousers hanger.

## Hanging Things Up:

There's no trick to hanging up clothes—just routine precautions that will keep them in better shape.

**Suit:** You can hang a skirt and jacket together on a single-barred hanger, but hang the jacket separately from the skirt if you are using a clamp hanger, which isn't shaped to fit the contours of the jacket's shoulders. When hanging a three-piece suit, the waistcoat and jacket should face the same way, and you must be careful not to ruffle the waistcoat when you put the jacket over it.

**Jacket:** Take everything out of the pockets so that there are no bulges to spoil its line. Leave the jacket unbuttoned—this makes it easier to put on again and allows air to circulate inside. Make sure the center of the collar lies against the crook of the hanger and that the shoulders sit evenly so that the jacket hangs straight. Then place the sleeves partially over the pockets, toward the front of the jacket, to keep them from being crushed.

**Waistcoat:** Make sure it's hanging smooth and straight and keep it unbuttoned, ready to wear.

**Trousers:** Hang them without a belt and with nothing in the pockets. When using a double-barred hanger, make sure that your trousers are centered as they will crease if they bunch up at one end. Both legs must lie smoothly, one directly above the other, when they hang over the bar. Having one leg lying slightly more to the left or right than the other leaves small parallel lines on the side of the leg that lies over the bar. Hang trousers about six inches above the knees so that the ankles and the waist are evenly balanced. Never hang them at the knees, which get the most wear.

When hanging two pairs of trousers on a hanger, face them in opposite directions so that the legs of each pair hang down on either side of the bar.

**Skirts:** When hanging a skirt, check that the waistband doesn't fold back on itself,

---

**Duties of the Valet**

Gentlemen are sometimes indifferent as to their clothes and appearance; it is the valet's duty...to select from the wardrobe such things as are suitable for the occasion, so that he may appear with scrupulous neatness and cleanliness... The routine of his evening duty is to have everything...in order that is required for his master's comforts.

— *Mrs. Beeton's Book of Household Management*, 1861

and if you are hanging two skirts on a single hanger, make sure that the one underneath is hanging smoothly.

**Pleats:** Odile Barbiere, who worked as a lady's maid for the same English lady for 45 years, recalls, "I used to tack the pleats in position every time I hung up my lady's skirt. It was one of the things you learned early on. It didn't take a minute to sew up. Then I would unpick the stitches before I laid the skirt out on her chair, ready for her to wear."

Nowadays, she recommends using clamp hangers. "They're easiest to use because you can just clamp the hanger over the skirt and the pleats will hang straight," she says. "But be careful not to ruffle the waistband and don't put more than one skirt on each hanger."

**Dresses:** Soft padded hangers are best for delicate fabrics. The crook of the hanger should be at the center of the collar so that the dress is evenly balanced. Always fasten buttons and zippers to help the dress keep its shape, and never let part of the sleeve stick out or it will crease. The cuffs should lie flat against the skirt. Fill out puffed or mutton-shaped sleeves with white tissue paper so that they stay looking crisp. Do the same for a bow — a little white tissue paper tucked inside a bow will keep it from being squashed.

Strapless evening dresses should be hung from the waistband, as should dresses in which the skirt's weight might pull the bodice out of shape. These include dresses with shoe-string shoulder straps and long dresses with heavy skirts. You can simply sew loops on the inside seams under the waistband, then turn the dress inside-out and hang it up like a skirt. Inside-out hanging is ideal for some other garments as well. When Chanel launched the Little Black Dress in the 1920s, it became a must in every fashionable woman's wardrobe. Sixty years later, black clothes are still a fashion staple and should be hung inside-out to protect the surface from dust or lint.

**Jeans:** In order to avoid a crease on the front and back of each leg, fold jeans lengthwise so that the back pockets press against each other. Then hang them up like any other pair of trousers.

**Coats:** Always use a sturdy hanger with rounded ends. Never hang coats up by the loop at the back of the neck for any length of time, which can cause an ugly bump below the collar and pull the coat out of shape. Hang it up like a jacket, evenly balanced on a single-barred hanger with nothing in the pockets and the sleeves hanging straight, a little in front of it.

**Hats:** Put one inside the other. If you wear hair lotion, line the inside of each hat with grease proof paper before stacking them.

**Ties:** Always untie the knot when you take off your tie so as not to leave a permanent crimp in it. Undo it carefully—tugging at the knot will stretch and twist the fabric. Put your tie away whenever you take it off to prevent creases and ensure that you'll be able to find it quickly when you want to wear it again. Knitted ties should always be folded as hanging them can stretch them out of shape. You can hang a tie over a tie rail on the inside of your closet door or lay a towel over the crossbar of a hanger and drape it over that. Or, you might choose to buy a tie rack with a separate bar for each tie. Never put ties one on top of the other over a single hook.

**Boots and Shoes:** Never store shoes one on top of the other as you risk scratching and dirtying the ones underneath. A shoe rack is an excellent way of storing shoes and you can easily make one yourself. All you need are a couple of curtain rods cut to the width of your closet. Place them about an inch and a half apart, one above the other. You can hook the heels over the top rail and rest the soles against the bottom one. Stand boots upright — never leave them on their sides. Always put trees in boots and shoes.

**Wet Clothes:** If you get caught in a downpour, don't come back and dry your clothes over a radiator or near a fire unless you absolutely have to. All fabrics need to be dried naturally to retain their proper shape. 'Naturally' means slowly and away from direct heat. If a fur jacket or a coat gets wet in a shower, shake the water off before hanging the garment in a cool, dry place. Put it away only when it's completely dry. A little rain or snow won't harm fur, but take it to your furrier for special attention if it's really soaked through.

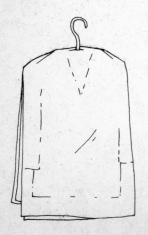

## Leather, Suede and Fur

**Leather and Suede:** Leather garments come in two finishes — smooth and suede — and both should be stored the same way. Hang leather jackets and coats on wooden hangers and protect them from dust by hanging white tissue over the crook of the hanger (see illustration) or by covering them with a cloth garment bag. Never use a plastic bag because air cannot circulate inside and a lack of air will eventually dry out the natural oils in the leather.

## How Maxwell Croft Cares for Fur

These do's and don'ts for the care and storage of fur were drawn up by well-known furrier *Maxwell Croft* of London.

### Do's

Use a broad shouldered padded hanger for coats and jackets.

Make sure that your fur has plenty of room in your closet so that it won't be crushed and marked by other garments.

Cover your fur with a loose cloth or cloth bag to protect it from dust. Some furs, such as fox, shed for a while when new, and a cloth bag will also prevent stray hairs from getting on the rest of your clothes.

Keep fur hats in a hat box or in a square box lined with white tissue paper. The box must be large enough not to press against the fur.

Hang fur boas over the second bar of a double-barred wooden hanger. Cover the boas with an old pillowcase placed over the crook of the hanger.

### Don'ts

Store fur in a plastic bag.

Put perfume directly onto fur. Its alcohol, which is difficult to remove even in cleaning, dries out the leather and stiffens the hairs.

Pin flowers or jewelry onto your fur — this can flatten and damage it.

Sit in a fur for any length of time, as this can crush it. You can lessen the strain by leaving your coat unfastened.

Drive long distances wearing a fur. Friction caused by certain types of car upholstery will make the fur shed.

Wear a shoulder bag. The strap will rub against the fur and flatten it.

# Folding Clothes

**Folding Clothes:** Fold anything that hanging might stretch out of shape, such as sweaters, knitwear, chiffon and evening dresses cut on the bias. (When a garment has been cut on the bias, the pattern has been cut diagonally across the vertical and horizontal grains and material. This results in an uneven distribution of weight and gives the fabric a tendency to sag.) Fine materials should be wrapped in white tissue paper before folding. You can lay a delicate dress face down on a couple of sheets of tissue and fold it as for packing. Put tissue between the folds and over the back of the dress before laying it face up in a drawer or on a shelf.

Shirts and blouses take up too much space hanging in a closet so it's more sensible to arrange them on shelves or in a chest of drawers.

**Organizing Yourself:** Messy drawers and shelves result when you can't decide what to wear and you jumble everything up as you look through clothes. The solution is to arrange garments so that each can be seen easily. This allows you to think out your color scheme in advance and remove the item you want without upsetting the rest of the pile. Separate garments according to use. Keep underwear and nightwear together. Have knitted ties and hosiery in one place, keep pantyhose in a shoe-tidy bag in your closet, and roll up socks and pop them in a pretty wicker basket left under a bedroom chair.

**Shirts and Blouses:** If you have the space, spread them out so that they overlap and allow you to remove one without dislodging the rest. Mark Fairweather likes to arrange a separate pile for each color when he unpacks for royal guests. "I put checked shirts, blue striped shirts, collarless shirts and evening shirts all into their own pile," he says. But when storage space is limited, it's best to create a gradual stack — one shirt over the other — so that part of each shirt is visible and you can easily see which is which.

Place shirts in a drawer with the collars away from you, and avoid handling the collar when you pull it out. Always remove shirts on top of the one you want instead of just pulling your choice out from under the others and upsetting the pile. It's easy to replace the neatly stacked pile of shirts. And don't bury a worn shirt in a drawer full of freshly laundered ones. Leave it on top of a clean pile so that you will wear it within the next couple of days.

**Pantyhose:** Line drawers and shelves with paper to keep pantyhose from snagging on splinters. Keep garter belts separately in your lingerie drawer with your stockings.

**Underwear/Men:** Men's undershirts and boxer shorts should be folded in their own piles. If you also have briefs and bikini style underpants, keep those together.

**Lingerie/Women:** Arrange your drawer to suit your preference. You can keep white briefs separately from colored or patterned ones or mix them up together, keep matching bras and pants next to each other or have all your bras in one pile, folded in half with one cup inside the other. Fold slips, camisoles and vests and keep them together or in separate piles. Do either with nighties and pajamas. Scented sachets in the drawer will keep everything fragrant.

*"A lady's maid would call her lady first thing in the morning — or rather, at the time she liked to be called. You would draw the curtains, pick up all the clothes she had worn the night before, and tidy the room and bed. The lady would get up and go into the bathroom, and you would order her breakfast. You waited for her to come back, and she would go back to bed and eat breakfast. You would leave her then, taking her clothes away to wash them."*
— Mlle. Elise Gaubert

# How to Fold a Shirt

Shirts are so well folded when they come back from the laundry that all you need to do is remove the wrapper. It is, however, very simple to fold a shirt after laundering it yourself or when putting it away for a second wearing.

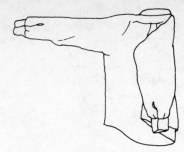

**3.** Fold the first sleeve from the shoulder to the shirttails. Never fold sleeves across the back of a shirt, because that causes a bump at the sides and in the middle.

**2.** Fold one side in a third of the way toward the back.

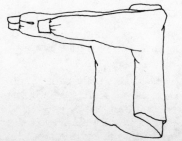

**1.** Fasten the middle button to keep the sides in position before laying the shirt face down.

**4.** Repeat on the second side. The second sleeve will lie partly over the first.

**5.** Fold the tails of a man's shirt up over the cuffs to keep them clean. Most women's shirts aren't long enough for this to be necessary.

**6.** Fold the shirt crosswise so that the end of the shirt reaches the edge of the collar.

**7.** Lay it face up on your drawer or shelf.

## How to Fold Socks and Ties

### Socks:

You can either roll socks up in a ball or fold them so that they are ready to slip over your feet.

**1.** Turn the first sock inside-out.

**2.** Put your hand inside it and pull the toe and heel up into the sock.

**3.** Do the same with the second one.

**4.** Keep the pair together by rolling the bottom of the first sock a couple of inches over the second sock.

### Ties:

Wool ties should be folded in half with the narrow end lying over the broad end. They can be folded in half again if necessary.

## How to Fold an Evening Shirt

Evening shirts worn with tuxedos and special white silk blouses should be stored in individual laundry bags or wrapped in white tissue paper.

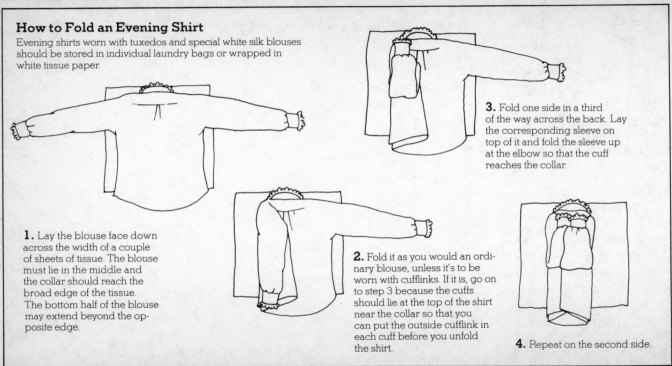

**1.** Lay the blouse face down across the width of a couple of sheets of tissue. The blouse must lie in the middle and the collar should reach the broad edge of the tissue. The bottom half of the blouse may extend beyond the opposite edge.

**2.** Fold it as you would an ordinary blouse, unless it's to be worn with cufflinks. If it is, go on to step 3 because the cuffs should lie at the top of the shirt near the collar so that you can put the outside cufflink in each cuff before you unfold the shirt.

**3.** Fold one side in a third of the way across the back. Lay the corresponding sleeve on top of it and fold the sleeve up at the elbow so that the cuff reaches the collar.

**4.** Repeat on the second side.

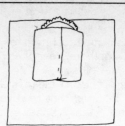

**5.** Fold the shirt crosswise as you would an ordinary shirt so that the hem reaches the edge of the collar.

**6.** Fold the tissue over the back of the shirt, then turn it over and tuck the tissue around the front of the shirt to make a tidy, protective package before putting it away.

## How to Fold a Sweater

There are two ways of folding a sweater. You can either fold it lengthwise in thirds, as you would a shirt, or fold it so that it lays flatter in your drawer. Fine sweaters should always be folded as flat as possible, with the sleeves folded across the back to minimize the folds and the possibility of creases.

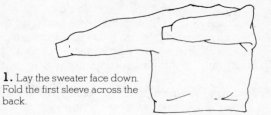

**1.** Lay the sweater face down. Fold the first sleeve across the back.

**2.** Fold the second sleeve across the back over the first sleeve.

**3.** Bring the bottom of the sweater to the inside edge of the neck.

**4.** Lay it facing upward on your drawer or shelf.

# Jewelry

**Jewelry/Men:** Because cufflinks are a practical and popular gift, most men tend to accumulate many pairs of them over the years. To keep track of them, keep them in a stud box along with your separate shirt collars, studs and tie pins.

"If you want your cufflinks and tie pins to look antique, don't clean them," advises Mark Fairweather. "They never become really dirty because they're covered by your jacket or kept in a stud box. If they are one hundred years old, they should look like it. Let them gather one hundred years worth of character and wear."

However, if you do want to clean cufflinks and tie pins, you can squeeze the juice of half a lemon into a cup and soak them in the juice for about 30 minutes. Rinse and dry them, and shine them up with a soft polishing cloth.

**Jewelry/Women:** It's a good idea to keep favorite pieces of jewelry in two boxes stored in different places — that way, if your home is broken into, the burglars may not find everything. Clean jewelry with a proprietary cleaner or in lukewarm water and mild detergent. Wash it in a bowl, not directly in the sink — too many small bits

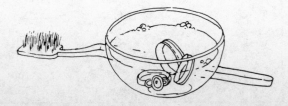

and pieces might be lost down the drain. Use a soft toothbrush to clean between the cracks, then rinse and dry. Use a polishing cloth to bring up a shine.

**Cigarette Lighters and Cases:** Remove fingermarks on gold and silver lighters and cases with a soft cloth impregnated with polish, such as Goddard's Long Term Silver Cloth.

**Gold Watch Straps:** Clean in lukewarm water with a mild detergent. You can gently scrub watch bands with a soft nailbrush to get rid of flakes of dried skin caught in them. For a bright shine, finish off with Goddard's Long Term Silver Cloth.

**Hairbrushes:** One of the greatest pleasures of owning silver-backed hairbrushes is seeing the way they shine when you lay them out on a dressing table. As soon as they begin to look tarnished, clean them with a soft cloth impregnated with polish. After you've removed the hairs from the bristles with a comb, you can dip the bristles in half an inch of lukewarm water and mild detergent. Don't let the base of the bristles get wet. Rinse in half an inch of clear water, shake off any excess water and allow the brush to dry naturally.

# Off Season

You can store clothes virtually any place as long as it's clean and dry. If clothes are stored where it's damp or humid, mildew will form and in time your clothes will rot. Always make sure that no water can seep into your storage area through badly sealed windows or skylights. Look for leaking pipes. Feel the walls and floor for dampness. If you are storing clothes in a walk-in closet, vacuum it. If there are shelves, dust them. Use high-gloss non-drip paint to brighten up closet walls and keep them clean. Then line your shelves with pretty contact paper.

**Dry Cleaning and Laundry:** It's essential to dry clean or launder your clothes before storing them to guard against moths and keep your clothes fresh until you want to wear them again. Before storing is the time to get zippers mended and buttons sewn on, but don't make major alterations. If you take up a hem or let out a seam at the end of a season, your shape, as well as fashion trends, may change by the time next season comes around again. It's best to wait and see.

**Moth Protection:** The more you use your closet and keep an eye on your clothes, the better your chances of flushing out any moths that might be settling there. Mothballs or aerosol moth repellent sprays are a good deterrent but leave the smell in your clothes. Pot pourri, on the other hand, is as effective as camphor but has a more attractive scent. A less expensive alternative is to tie together a small bunch of five or six bay leaves and hang them in your closet. Use a needle to thread a piece of cotton through the bottom of the leaves and hang them below the crooks of the hangers. Change the leaves every three or four months to keep them fresh. Bay leaves or pot pourri will also protect your clothes against silverfish, harmless insects about a quarter of an inch long.

**Garment Bags:** Drape a sheet over off-season clothes or use strong plastic or nylon dress bags with a zipper at the side to keep out the dust. It's also a good idea to keep fine evening clothes in a clothes bag, or to at least protect the shoulders and lapels by hanging a sheet of white tissue from the crook of the hanger.

## Long Term Storage

**Containers:** England's Royal Ballet drapes their costumes on nylon-covered rails with a green canvas waterproof cover over them. Some costumes stored in this fashion have lasted over 25 years. However, although theatrical costumes must be hung on rails for the sake of expediency, it's better to fold clothes away in a trunk because prolonged hanging can cause them to fade and lose their shape. A trunk that locks is more secure than a cardboard box or soft-walled luggage, which are likely to be flimsy and too small.

Clean the trunk first. Then pack everything according to its weight — heavier garments go at the bottom, lighter ones go on top. Put sachets of pot pourri between the layers of clothing and cover the top layer with white tissue paper. Seal the trunk with sticky tape to keep out dust. Check your trunk at least once a year to change the sachets and to make sure that everything is in good order.

You can use a single trunk for winter clothes, country clothes and tweed jackets. Pack lighter garments — summer clothes, smart suits, dresses and evening clothes — in a second trunk. You can have a separate trunk for shirts, sweaters and underwear, or keep them in a drawer wrapped in a sheet. Lay half of the sheet inside the drawer and let the other half hang outside; then put your shirts, underwear and sweaters in the drawer and cover them with the rest of the sheet. Tuck the sheet around the garments before closing the drawer.

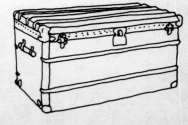

**Babies' Clothes:** These can last for generations provided they are correctly stored. "I have unpacked babies' clothes that I knitted over 30 years ago that are still as good as new," says English nanny Winifred Wilson, also known as Nanny Chadwyck-Healey because she has been with the Chadwyck-Healey family for over 20 years. "Everything must be washed and ironed before it's put away," she advises. "But never put away cotton that is starched because in time the starch will destroy the fabric and rust will appear." So however tempting it is to iron and starch a family christening robe—don't do it. Put it away 'rough dried,' a nanny's term for washing and lightly ironing it. Then wrap it in tissue and put it in a box.

When putting away babies' clothes, use white tissue paper to separate each item. You can keep babies' woolens in a plastic bag, but make sure there is no air in it by sucking out the air with a straw before you seal it. Keep cottons, woolens and linens in separate boxes that are tied with string and clearly marked. Keep the boxes in a closet and don't just forget about them until there is a new baby—check them once in a while.

**Furs:** Cold storage during the summer protects furs from moths and insects. The cool temperature, just above freezing, prevents the fur from drying out and the hairs from splitting so that the fur is in good condition when it's brought out to wear in the fall. Have your fur looked at by your furrier before you put it in storage. He can tell you if it needs professional cleaning. Depending on how often you wear it, your fur may need cleaning once a year or once every three years. Although fur doesn't show dirt it does feel sticky or grimy when it needs cleaning. Fur boas or hats need to be cleaned once every three or four years.

# PACKING WELL

"The minute a suitcase is opened you can tell whether or not a butler has packed it," says footman Mark Fairweather. "I have grown up with the knowledge of how to pack," he explains. "I first learned when I went to work at the age of 14 under Stanley Ager, the butler at St. Michael's Mount, a castle off the Cornish Coast of England. I have never seen a case packed properly by someone who doesn't have a butler. I always have to brush and press the clothes that guests have packed themselves because they are invariably squashed and crumpled on arrival. A butler has learned through experience how much you need to take and how it will fit into your case."

**Packing Lists:** Maureen Gavin, wardrobe mistress to England's Royal Ballet, says it's like moving house when the company goes on tour. "We pack for six or seven large productions," she says, "and we take everything we can — including soap powder, irons, ironing boards, a clothes washing machine and a couple of tumble driers."

For most of us, packing is a far simpler affair, one that requires only a few days of advance planning. Choose your clothes far enough in advance to allow time to wash or dry clean those garments that need it. Once you've decided which clothes you want to take, lay them out. Now, unless you're traveling by car and have unlimited space for luggage, put one third of your selection back in the closet — even if you wind up eliminating clothes that were specially cleaned for your trip. This old traveler's maxim keeps you from lugging clothes you don't need and leaves room in your suitcase for the souvenirs or presents you might want to bring back with you.

**Business Trips:** Assume that most of the people you'll be meeting with are only going to see you once. You can pack accordingly. However, it is always a good idea to pack a selection of colored, striped, and plain shirts so that you can alternate them with the same suit, giving your suit a slightly different look each time you wear it.

**Weekends with Friends:** A pair of jeans are a *must* on an informal weekend, and during the winter months remember to take waterproof boots. If you're invited for a formal weekend, you may need to bring a tuxedo or smart evening dress. In this instance, men and women traveling together should each bring their own medium-sized suitcase rather than attempt to force these two highly crushable items into one large bag.

Before World War II, an invitation to a weekend house party meant taking at least three cases, as a change of clothes was required for virtually every activity and almost every meal. Packing was elaborate even when the wealthy went home to their country estates. "We left London every weekend for the country," recalls Mademoiselle Elise Gaubert. "I sat in the front of the car with the chauffeur and my lady sat in the back. But a lady's maid was never at ease; you were always worried. Your major worry was your lady's jewels — were they safe, and had you packed the right ones? Then you were worried that you had forgotten to pack something. Basic essentials, such as make-up, were duplicated in both the London and country homes, but each dress had its own matching bag, gloves, shoes, and parasol, and if

*"The last years before the first World War...From March or April the season of weekend house-parties was under way. Every Friday evening or more usually Saturday morning the upper classes would pour out of London to congregate 20, 30 or 40 strong in the country houses within a railway-journey's distance of the capital, to shoot, fish, hunt; play golf, tennis and after-dinner games; of which adultery was the most popular; or to conduct the business of the country in dignified seclusion."*
— Philip Ziegler, *Diana Cooper*

you forgot to pack one of those things they would murder you."

**Air Travel:** Always pack a sweater in your hand luggage as the air conditioning in the plane tends to be chilly. And try to take all of your essentials—the items you simply can't do without—on board with you, just in case your luggage is lost. In fact, on short trips you can entirely eliminate the problem of straying baggage and save yourself a tedious wait on arrival by packing all your things into a carry-on bag and a garment bag that can be hung in the plane's closet. Roomy pocketbooks and briefcases are a good luggage supplement for small items.

# Arranging and Folding

Packing a suitcase is like packing the trunk of a car — you have to think about how to fit everything into a limited space. Each layer of clothes must lie as flat as possible, and it's a good idea to fill up all the gaps between clothes with small items so that the clothing is held firm. There should be enough pressure on every level to hold the clothes still, but not so much that the clothes are crushed.

Folding garments can cause creases, so the fewer folds you make in your clothes, the better. If a garment is badly crumpled when you unpack it, shake out the creases before you hang it up and they will probably fall out.

**Tissue Paper and Polythene Bags:** The most effective way to prevent creasing is to cover the garment with a polythene garment bag or even the plastic bag you get from the dry cleaners. The air in the bag which surrounds the garment acts as a

### Airline Baggage Allowance

The standard airline baggage allowance is two cases that can weigh up to 70 lbs. and a carry-on bag, provided all three pieces conform to specific measurements. The carry-on bag must measure less than 45 inches in length, width, and depth. Measure its length from end to end, the width from the front to the back, and the depth from the bottom to the top. Add up these three measurements. If the total is less than 45 inches, it's within the allowance.

The two other cases go in the hold. The largest piece of luggage cannot exceed 62 inches in length, width, and depth, and the total measurements of both cases cannot be more than 106 inches.

cushion so that no weight bears down on it from the other items in the suitcase. For extra protection, Mark Fairweather suggests putting white tissue between each fold in the garment before placing it in a plastic bag. "Always use white tissue," he warns. "It won't tear easily, and more importantly, the dye from colored tissue may get onto your clothes."

**Dresses/Fine Fabrics:** Evening dresses, silk dresses, and fine materials need tissue paper before they are placed in a plastic bag for packing. Lay the tissue paper down the back of the dress. (You may need to use two sheets so that it runs all the way down the center from the collar to the hem.) If the dress has puffed sleeves, scrunch up a ball of tissue and slip it inside the sleeves to help them keep their shape. Put the tissue under frills and inside bows to keep them from being squashed. Once all the protective tissue is in place, simply fold the dress according to the instructions.

**Jeans:** You fold them as you would any pair of trousers or, because they are sturdy, you can roll them from the cuffs to the waistband and use them to fill in the gaps in your suitcase.

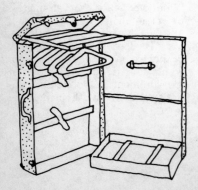

**Shirts and Sweaters:** Pack a new shirt or a shirt that has just returned from the laundry in its bag. Fold shirts as described on page 60. Fold a sweater as you would a shirt, or fold the sleeves straight across the back as described on page 63.

**Hat, Scarf and Gloves:** When packing a felt hat, stuff the crown with small soft odds and ends to keep it from being crushed. Make sure the brim is supported by the packing underneath it. Fold a neck scarf rather than rolling it, and pack gloves flat, palm against palm.

**Shoes:** Use shoe bags or wrap shoes in white tissue paper to protect your clothing. Pack low-heeled shoes with the uppers, not the soles, facing each other and place them toe to heel. Place high heeled shoes so that the uppers face the side of the case and the heel faces inward. Wrap a pair of socks around the heels to protect them.

**Sundries/Women:** Very small containers of make-up — the kind given away as samples or gift offers at cosmetic counters — are excellent for traveling.

**Sundries/Men:** A shaving kit with a drawstring takes up very little space as long as you squeeze out the air to make it as thin as possible.

**Laundry:** Rolling dirty clothes in a ball takes up too much space. Pack laundry flat at the bottom of your case and lay a worn shirt over the top of it to keep it together, or cover it with a plastic bag.

## Fitting Things In

Pack heavy casual clothes and bulky unbreakable things first. Pack delicate garments on top of them. The following list of items is arranged in the order that they should be packed.

**Shoes:** Fit them in first in the corners.

**Jeans:** Put them in next along with heavy-weight skirts and casual slacks.

(continued on page 80)

# How Mark Fairweather Folds a Suit

It's easiest to fold a suit, or any other garment, on a bed or bedside table before putting it in your case.

**Jacket:** There are a number of ways to fold a jacket, but this method is the simplest, has the least folds and makes the flattest package.

**1.** When you take your jacket out of the closet it should be unbuttoned, ready for wear, and ready for packing. Lay it face up and make sure that the collar is flat and the shoulders are squared.

**2.** Pull the buttonhole side of the jacket so that it overlaps the buttons by five or six inches. The side seams that run from under the armhole to the bottom of the jacket or to the jacket pocket should lie in a smooth, straight line on either side of the jacket.

**3.** Fold the first sleeve over the lapels toward the opposite shoulder. The jacket should lie flat and it must not pull under the armhole.

**4.** Do the same with the second sleeve, crossing it over the first sleeve.

**5.** Bring the bottom of the jacket up to the shoulder, so that it's folded in half. Gently pull each end of the jacket over the outside edges of the sleeves. Put crushable fabrics inside a plastic bag. Lay the jacket face up in your case.

**Waistcoat:**

**1.** Lay the unbuttoned waistcoat flat, right side up.

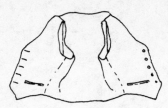

**2.** Fold it lengthwise on the back seam, preserving the natural fold under each armhole. The two lower points will overlap.

**3.** Fold along the side seam beneath each armhole. If your waistcoat is small enough you can pack it just like this. If not, follow step 4.

**4.** Fold the waistcoat in half crossways, so that the shoulders and armholes lie on the broad body of the waistcoat.

**Trousers:**

**1.** Trousers are folded at the base of the seat when you take them off the hanger, so all you need to do is to lay them flat. Empty the pockets and fold the linings away from the front of the trousers so as not to interfere with the crease.

**2.** If you have a wide girth, fold the back of the waistband down and toward the front at an angle, as illustrated.

**3.** The last step is to fold the trousers so that the legs reach the waistband.

## Skirts:

Fold a flared skirt in a rectangular shape to line up with the rest of your packing.

**1.** Lay the skirt face down.

**2.** Fold in one side of the skirt to make a straight line from the waistband to the hem.

**3.** Repeat on the other side.

**4.** Fold the skirt from the hem to the waistband.

For fine materials, put tissue paper in the center of the skirt before you fold it in at the sides (step 2). Slip a plastic bag over the completely folded skirt.

**Dresses:**

**1.** Lay the dress flat, face down.

**2.** Fold one side back about 1/3 of the way to the center of the dress. The flare of the skirt should be folded in so that the outside edge is an even line from top to bottom.

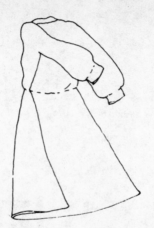

**3.** Fold the sleeve back over the first fold so that it falls from the shoulder to the waist in a straight line.

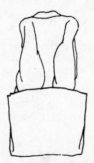

**5.** Fold the skirt from the hem to the waist.

**6.** Then fold the dress at the waist, so the second fold reaches the bottom of the collar.

**4.** Fold in the other side; lay the second flare on top of the first flare and fold back the sleeve.

**7.** If it crumples easily, slip the folded dress into a plastic bag. Lay the dress face up in your case.

## How Mlle. Gaubert Protects Pleats

Pleated skirts are always difficult to pack because the pleats lose their shape so easily, especially if the skirt is made of a heavy fabric like wool or linen. You can keep pleats looking crisp by using bobby pins (kirbigrips) to hold the fabric in place. Use new pins that won't rust and place them under each pleat to hold the fold in position without marking the right side of the material.

1. Place the grips under each pleat.

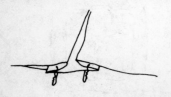

**Shirts and Sweaters:** Most can go near the middle of the bag—silk and evening shirts should go near the top. Protect shirts by putting them front to front, placing the collar of one at the bottom fold of the other. Pack angora, cashmere, and silk jersey as flat as possible. Angora sheds easily so put it in a plastic bag to protect the rest of your clothes. Use shetland, lambswool or acrylic sweaters to cushion breakables and to fill the gaps in your bag.

**Suits:** Suits should always be packed near the top of your case, above everyday shirts and sweaters, because nothing looks worse than a crumpled suit. A creased shirt is less obvious because most of it is usually hidden under your jacket or sweater. Creases usually fall out of a sweater from the warmth of your body after you've put it on. Arrange one suit on top of another, starting with heavy woolen fabrics and ending with lighter weights. Pack the trousers or skirt first, followed by the waistcoat and jacket, so that you can put each garment directly onto the hanger in the proper order as soon as you unpack it.

**Waistcoat:** Lay it flat between the trousers and jacket.

**Dresses:** More delicate dresses should be placed at the top where they won't get crushed, but heavy corduroy or woolen dresses can be packed before suits.

**Jacket:** Don't let the collar press against the sides of the suitcase—it will get crushed. Face it toward the middle of your packing, or toward the handle. Since the bag can't stand on the side with the handle, the collar won't be pressed against the wall of the suitcase when it's upright.

**Ties:** Pack silk ties flat in a parcel of tissue paper near the top of your bag. Lay the rest of your ties between your underwear and shirts.

**Underwear:** Women can use lingerie bags or loose articles to fill up spaces and men can pack underwear flat to fill gaps.

**Dressing Gown:** Lay it face up and fold it like a jacket. Fold it from the hem to the waist and from the waist to the collar. Use dressing gowns made of silk or flimsy material to spread over the top of your packing to keep it tight and to protect it from dust.

**Raincoat:** If you are carrying it over your arm, carry it inside out to keep it clean. When packing a raincoat, fold it as you would fold a jacket for a suitcase but fold it crosswise from the hem to the waist and from the waist to the collar.

## Hanging Bags

Hanging bags are designed to be light-weight and easy to pack, not roomy. Don't overfill them or you will crush your clothes. If you think there's enough space in the bag for a third suit, leave it out and substitute a pair of slacks or a jacket instead.

Start by laying the bag on the floor or on a bed. Take your clothes from the closet and shake out the creases. Make sure that the clothes are arranged properly on their hangers and that they are perfectly flat when you put them in the bag.

**Shoes:** Put shoes in first, tucked into the corners. (They should be at the top of the bag after it's been folded up, otherwise you will have a large bump in the middle.) At

**2.** Push grips in so that they don't stick out.

You can protect a pleated silk skirt or an accordion pleated skirt by putting it inside an old stocking. Lay each pleat on top of the other so that the skirt forms a tight cylinder. Put the stocking over it to keep the pleats together and tuck it in your suitcase.

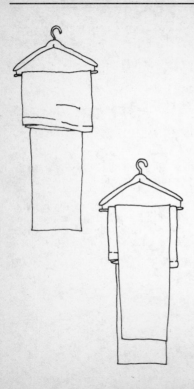

the finish, they will lie above your jacket shoulders, with the toes pointing toward the handle. The soles of low-heeled shoes can press against the case with the uppers facing inward, but do the opposite with high-heeled shoes. The uppers must press against the side of the case with the soles facing inward to protect them.

**Suits:** Suits are one of the last items to put in the bag. You can hang the trousers, waistcoat and jacket on the same hanger — the trousers go on first, then the waist-coat, then the jacket hangs over the waistcoat. You can minimize creasing by covering the suit with a plastic bag and hanging it with its back toward the garment bag's zipper.

**Trousers:** They should be centered on the hanger. Mark Fairweather says that the waistband should hang about 10 inches below the bar so that the bag only folds the lower part of the legs.

Alternatively, you can fold the legs back over the trousers and lay the ends over the bar. If you are hanging two pairs of trousers, hang them in opposite directions over the bar. If you are folding the legs back over the bar, the legs of the top pair should hang longer than the bottom pair to hold both trousers steady.

Jeans and casual slacks can go in first behind your suits.

**Skirts:** Fold in the sides to make an even line from the top of the waistband to the hem. Cover fine materials with a plastic bag. Don't hang more than two skirts on the same hanger.

**Waistcoat:** Take the buttonholes a third of the way over the pocket on the opposite side. The end points should overlap and the waistcoat should hang flat.

**Jacket:** The pockets should be empty with the pocket flaps lying outside. Leave the jacket unbuttoned and center the collar against the crook of the hanger. Bring the buttonholes a third of the way over the opposite side so that the jacket will fit in neatly without folding. If you are not covering your suit with a plastic bag, it is important that the sleeves are hanging straight, a little in front of the jacket. Then you will have to lay the jacket face up in the hanging bag.

**Dresses:** Make sure that it's centered on the hanger with the sleeves hanging a little in front of the skirt. Carefully place it face up in the bag. You may need to fold up the bottom of a long dress to fit it in. If the dress will crumple easily, line the bodice and sleeves with tissue and slip it in a plastic bag before putting it in the case.

**Shirts and Sweaters:** Pack them folded as flat as possible to reduce creasing and conserve space. Pop folded shirts in the outside pocket of the bag. Wrap fine shirts in tissue paper, or better still, keep them in a shirt bag. Use sweaters to fill gaps. Cover your heavy clothing with your longest sweater to keep everything in place. Tuck any extra material down the sides of the bag.

**Underwear and Hosiery:** Fill gaps with lingerie bags. Pack loose underwear flat in the side pockets and put rolled socks inside your shoes.

**Sundries:** Because of its compact design and flimsy build, a hanging bag offers less protection for breakables than any other piece of luggage. The safest place for fragile items are the corners near the handle where no weight is put on the case. Put a man's shaving kit or woman's make-up bag in one of these corners.

**Dressing Gown:** Unless you are planning to bring a raincoat, pack this last to hold your packing together and to keep out dust.

## Grips and Backpacks

**Grips:** Soft-sided grips are ideal for traveling light and for carrying casual clothes. They are wonderfully expansive, and should be packed tightly so that they don't get droopy.

The trick is to fold everything to the shape of the bag, which is why a jacket is folded differently for a grip than for a standard suitcase. If the grip is large enough, you can fold all your other clothes as you would fold them for a standard bag. If your grip is too small, pack dresses and skirts flat, but roll slacks, jeans, sweaters and shirts. Use sweaters, underwear and hosiery to fill gaps and cushion breakables. Roll socks and stuff them inside shoes at the bottom of the grip. Tuck your shaving kit or make-up bag down one of the sides close to the top so it's within easy reach. Wear or carry your raincoat and use your dressing gown to cover your packed clothes. On your return trip, roll up each item and use it to fill gaps in your packing.

**Backpacks:** A backpack has a rugged style all its own, with the added advantage of leaving your hands free for other tasks. Backpacks are comfortable to wear as long as you are not groaning beneath their weight, so always take the minimum. Roll up everything, including shirts, sweaters and underwear.

## How to Fold a Jacket for a Grip:

The idea is to preserve the natural folds at the waistline and the seams.

**1.** Empty out the pockets. Lay the jacket flat, lining side down. Turn the collar up so it lies flat. (It's reinforced, so it will not crease.)

**4.** Fold the jacket along the center back seam, bringing the lapels together. The jacket is now long and thin, and there is a natural fold under each armhole.

**2.** Fold up both sleeves at the elbow so the tip of the cuffs reach the outside edge of the shoulders.

**3.** Turn back the sides of the jacket to the center back seam, which should just be visible between them.

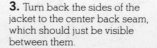

**5.** Fold up at the waist. To make it fit your grip, tuck in any extra material from the coattails between the folds of the jacket.

# SHOE AND LEATHER CARE

## Boots and Shoes

"The investment in buying a pair of excellent shoes makes sense only if you look after them well and keep them clean," says John Lobb, a director of *John Lobb Ltd.*, London's most exclusive shoemaker on St. James Street. The firm charges about £450 (approximately $700) for a pair of custom-made shoes and £1,000 (approximately $1,600) for a pair of hand-made boots, both of which have been known to last more than a lifetime when properly looked after. "We get shoes coming back for repair that are 15, 20, 40, even 100 years old," Lobb says proudly. But whether you are trying to ensure a lifetime investment in a pair of *John Lobb* shoes or simply trying to get your money's worth, the rules for looking after them are the same.

## Do's and Don'ts
### Do's
Regularly polish all shoes to feed the leather and give them a shine. Use a shoe horn — or even the back of a spoon handle — to help slip your heels into your shoes without pressing down on the shoe's back. Always put shoe trees into your shoes as

soon as you take them off. Shoes stretch out of shape after supporting the weight of your body all day, and putting trees in them while the shoes are still warm and malleable brings them back into shape. Wooden shoe trees are best because they hold the shoe rigid, absorb perspiration, and allow the leather to breathe after the shoe has become wet. If you don't have shoe trees, you can stuff a pair of rolled-up socks into the toe part of the shoe, which needs more support than the heel. Always put trees in the toe of boots and in the legs to prevent them from sagging. You can buy special, tall boot trees or make cylinders for the legs out of cardboard.

### Don'ts

Don't wear the same pair of shoes every day or you will wear them out. Give them a day off to rest and air because, even in cold weather, shoes absorb a lot of moisture from your feet. Don't let the heels on your shoes get run down too far. It looks unattractive and more importantly, it can permanently ruin the shape of your shoes by altering the way your body weight settles into them.

Never store shoes one on top of the other, as the soles of the top shoes will scratch and dirty the ones below. Never leave boots or shoes near heat. Always allow damp shoes to dry slowly and naturally because heat cracks leather.

## Washing Shoes

You can wash tough outdoor leather shoes, such as heavy brogues and walking shoes, to remove mud and wash out salt marks from the sea or from walking on a sidewalk where salt has been laid down following a snow storm. You can also wash shoes to get rid of foot odors, but only if absolutely necessary because in time water will damage the leather. To wash muddy shoes, gently scrape off the worst of the mud with the side of a knife. Then use a coarse bristle brush to scrub off the remaining mud. (If you use a rag, you'll only rub mud into the cracks.) Use a sponge or nailbrush to clean the inside.

Shoes with leather heels (recognizable by the thin leather bands running around them) can be immersed in cold or lukewarm water with a drop of ammonia added to it. Stand the shoes upside down for a few minutes to allow the water to drain. Mop up the remaining water with an old rag, and then pack the shoes tightly with newspaper to absorb moisture and to help them keep their shape.

**Drying:** Dry your shoes naturally, preferably in the open air. After 12 hours in the air remove the newspaper and repack them with fresh, dry newspaper. After another 12 hours, discard the paper to allow the air to circulate inside. When the shoes are nearly dry, put trees in them and rub a little cream polish into the leather to condition it. When the shoes are completely dry, rub them with a dry cloth to remove any cream that hasn't been absorbed. This will bring up a dullish shine. Then, start polishing again with a fresh smear of polish.

**Fine Leathers:** Most women's shoes—in fact, any shoe with a smooth leather finish—must be treated carefully. Brush out any grit caught between the sole and upper with a soft brush. Get rid of the smell of stale perspiration by wiping the inside with a damp sponge or soft nailbrush that has been dipped in a bowl of warm water with a drop of ammonia added. Remove marks on crocodile shoes, pastel-colored shoes, and silver and gilt shoes by lightly sponging them with a swab of damp cotton wool that has been dipped in a bowl of soapy water. Replace the trees and allow your shoes to dry naturally. When dry, polish them.

# Shoe Kit

**Polish:** There are all kinds of polishes on the market. But cream polish (sold in jars) or wax polish (sold in cans) will shine shoes and hide scuff marks far better than spray-on polish or saddle-soap. Cream polishes and wax polishes are available in colors that match a vast range of shades of leather. Cream polish feeds leather, preserves it, and keeps it supple. Wax polish will bring up a shine faster than cream and is more water resistant. Many people find it best to use wax on hard-wearing leathers and cream on the rest of their shoes. When using wax, be careful to avoid a build-up of polish, which leaves a dark mark on the shoe. If this happens, rub a transparent wax such as Kiwi Light Tan into the spot with a corner of a dust rag wrapped around your forefinger. Press hard. If the color of the leather becomes too light, rub the area again with a wax polish that is a shade darker than your shoes. At the very least you need a soft cloth to bring up a shine after you work the polish into

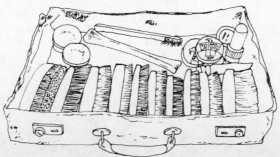

Thomas Hill's Shoe Care Kit

### Duties of the Footman

The footman is expected to rise early, in order to get through all his dirty work before the family are stirring. Boots and shoes, and knives and forks, should be cleaned, lamps in use trimmed, his master's clothes brushed, the furniture rubbed over; so that he may put aside his working dress, tidy himself, and appear in a clean jacket to lay the cloth and prepare breakfast for the family.

— *Mrs. Beeton's Book of Household Management*, 1861

your shoes. An old flannel vest is ideal. Finish off with a chamois leather. A genuine oil-dressed animal skin will work better than a simulated one.

You need a clean dust cloth to dust shoes that you haven't worn for a while. And if you are using a cream polish, you will have to put it on the shoe with a rag or soft dust cloth because the polish will fall between the bristles of a brush.

**Brushes:** You can buy a specially designed, long-handled, circular brush for applying polish, or you can use an ordinary polishing brush. If you do use a polishing brush as an applicator, make sure you mark it so you can distinguish it from the brush you actually use for polishing.

Never allow your polishing brushes to become wet — the bristles will turn soft and mushy. They need cleaning occasionally to remove the excess polish that gets caught between the bristles. To do this, wrap a double layer of brown paper (dull side up) around the edge of a table, and rub the brush up and down the paper. Always store your applicator and polishing brushes separately to avoid accidentally transferring polish from the bristles of the applicator to the polisher. Arrange them so that the bristles of one brush lie against the wooden handle of the other.

## To Polish

Your shoes should be free of dirt or dust before you begin polishing them. Remove the laces on lace-ups, and cover bows and decorations with saran wrap (cling film) to prevent polish from getting on them. It's easiest to polish your shoes on a table that has been covered with newspaper. Whenever possible, keep the trees in each shoe as you polish. If you don't have trees, put your hand as far into the shoe as feels comfortable.

**Coldstream Guards' Spit and Polish:** "By bulling your boots, using a bit of spit and polish, you get a fantastic shine and feed the leather as well," says Thomas Hill, an Officer's Servant in Britain's Coldstream Guards during World War II, and valet and butler to Sir Richard Boughey for over 30 years. "The more you polish, the greater the shine, and the better it is for the shoe," Hill says. "I enjoy cleaning shoes and like to spend hours and hours shining so that by the time I've finished you can see your face in it.

"New boots and shoes don't shine up as well as ones that have accumulated years of polish," he adds. "Ideally you should get rid of the polish on new leathers and start afresh with your own polish. One of the best ways of doing this is to go on a long country walk in your new boots or shoes and get them caked with mud and clay. Then wash off the dirt and leave them to dry in their own time before you begin working on them."

**Boning:** This is an old-fashioned technique used mostly on wax leather hunting boots and walking shoes. Blacking was applied with a stick and the shoes were rubbed with a piece of bone from the foreleg of a sheep or deer. The friction created by the bone rubbing against the leather brought out the natural oils and created an outstanding shine. It pressed out the scratches and made a new surface. Only shoes made of wax calf, an extremely tough leather, are strong enough to withstand boning. Most modern boots and shoes are made of box calf, a sturdy leather that can easily be cleaned by more conventional methods.

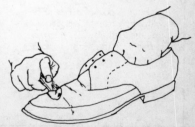

In the days when the well-to-do had a large staff to look after their wardrobes,

(continued on page 95)

## Coldstream Guards' Spit and Polish

Thomas Hill uses Kiwi Wax polish — he uses the spit and polish technique only on hard-wearing leathers such as walking shoes, stout slip-ons and leather riding boots.

**2.** From now on use a dust cloth to put on your polish. Wrap a corner around your first and second fingers. Tighten it to make a firm pad to rub the polish in with by twisting the rest of the cloth into a tight coil. Hold the loose ends of the cloth in the palm of your hand.

**1.** Put the polish on one shoe with a brush. Let the polish soak into the leather while you work polish onto the second shoe.

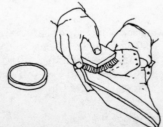

**3.** Put a smear of polish on the cloth. Never scoop polish out of a can — just dab the cloth onto the surface.

**5.** Never spit after eating sweets or chocolate because the sweetness in your saliva makes the leather too greasy. Instead, put a few drops of cold water in the upturned lid of your polishing can. Dab your dust cloth in the water to moisten it — but don't let it become too damp — before rubbing the shoe.

**6.** Spit and polish on each part of the shoe, except the heel, until you have brought up a bright shine.

**4.** Rub the polish into the toe with a circular motion. When you feel the polish dragging, spit on the shoe, as though spitting out an orange pip. Rub the area again with your cloth. Add only a tiny amount of polish to your cloth after it has rubbed off onto the shoe. Don't add too much polish or you'll never get a proper shine.

**7.** Polish the shoe with your polishing brush. Use light strokes — don't scrub at the shoe. Scrubbing is bad for the leather and will lessen the shine. A right-handed person usually polishes counterclockwise, but either method works well. Brush the heel and go around the shoe three or four times.

**8.** Finish off by rubbing each shoe with a chamois leather or make a pad out of a soft polishing cloth and polish it up with that.

## How Thomas Hill Cleans Suede Shoes:

"I don't believe in washing suede shoes, however muddy they are, as I think this makes them shiny. I like to let the mud dry and then to brush it off with a dandy brush, the type of brush used for grooming horses."

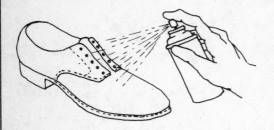

**1.** Spray the surface with a suede cleaner, following the instructions on the can.

**2.** When the cleaner has dried into a fine powder, brush it off with a wire brush. Brush around the shoe with a circular motion in a clockwise direction to bring up the nap. (Counterclockwise brushing will flatten suede.)

**3.** If the nap is worn, you can restore it by placing your shoes near a boiling kettle. The steam will raise the nap. Allow the suede to dry before brushing with your wire brush.

valets would spend hours boning their employers' boots and shoes, while shoemakers such as *Lobb*'s employed two or three people for the sole purpose of boning customers' shoes. But there were short-cuts, and one of these is still sometimes used in the army. A soldier may warm a spoon handle near the fire and then rub it lightly over his boot instead of using a bone. The heat draws out the wax and brings up a fantastic shine. However, since this technique, when repeated a number of times also cracks the leather, it is officially forbidden.

**Fine Leathers:** Thomas Hill uses Meltonian Cream on most women's shoes, court shoes, Gucci slip-ons and all soft leathers.
**1.** Use a soft rag and take care to apply only a small amount of cream polish — too much can stick in the seams and mark the shoe.
**2.** Lightly rub the cream in with a circular motion to allow it to get into all the cracks.
**3.** Start with the toe and work around the shoe. Don't forget the heel.
**4.** Fold your cream polishing cloth four times to make it into a soft pad. Hold it in the palm of your hand and lightly buff each shoe with it.
**5.** Finish off with a clean chamois. If the chamois has brown or black polish on it, use it only for dark brown or black shoes as it will mark lighter colors.

**Crocodile and Lizard Shoes:** Rub with a soft cloth after each wearing to remove dust and particles. Lizard shoes do not need polishing and crocodile shoes need only an occasional application of neutral shoe cream. Make sure the heels do not wear down so far that the leather is marked.

**Canvas Shoes:** You can brush them with an ordinary clothes brush and remove spots with a canvas cleaner following the manufacturer's instructions.

**Plastic Shoes:** Plastics are easy to care for and need only be wiped with a damp cloth.

**Patent Leather:** Wipe with a damp cloth and allow to dry before applying a neutral shoe cream or vaseline to nourish the leather and clean the shoe. Polish with a soft cloth.

Scratches on patent leather can often be disguised with a light application of colorless nail varnish. Let it dry completely, then rub with a soft dust cloth. To avoid scratches, store shoes wrapped up in a shoe bag. Leave them in a warm place (away from direct heat) to soften the leather before wearing in cold weather if you have not worn them for some time.

**Children's Shoes:** Use a renovating liquid or the same shade of paint to hide scuff marks if polish is ineffective. Before painting, clean off grease and dirt with a cloth that has been immersed in detergent and lukewarm water. Wring out the cloth so that it's just damp when you rub it over the shoe. Allow the shoe to dry. Then apply a small amount of paint with a paintbrush to the worn leather. Use matching polish to nourish the leather after the paint has dried.

## Leather Goods

**Suitcases:** Wipe dust and dirt off the case with a damp cloth, and remove dark stains with a cloth that has been dipped in a bowl of hot water and a mild detergent. Work from the center of the mark to its edges, rubbing gently with a circular motion. Let the case dry for a few minutes before going over it a couple of times with a damp sponge and saddle soap, which polishes and conditions the leather. When dry, polish with a chamois.

**Handbags:** Empty out all the bits and pieces that have collected in the bottom of your bag and lightly dust the inside to get rid of fine powder and fluff. Use a damp cloth to wipe off fingermarks on the outside. When it's dry, use a cream that matches the color of the bag. Work the cream into the leather with a clean cloth, but use only a small amount or your bag may become oily and mark your clothes. Polish with a polishing cloth and finish off with a chamois.

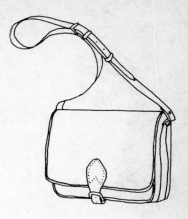

## Leather Garments

Follow the instructions that come with the garment, and have it professionally cleaned (including re-tinting and re-oiling) every three to four years. In between cleanings you can wipe it with a moist sponge and smear of saddle soap. Allow it to dry naturally and rub it with a clean chamois before putting it away.

Suede garments need careful treatment. When suede looks worn, hang the garment in the bathroom and run a hot shower. The steam absorbed into the leather will lift up the fibers. When it's dry, brush in a circular motion with a wire brush.

You can take out grease stains by sprinkling Johnson's Baby Powder into the mark. Leave for 20 minutes or so to allow the powder to absorb the grease and then brush away the powder with a wire brush.

# SPOT AND STAIN REMOVAL

Spills are inevitable. You are going to spill something — food, drink or some other substance — on favorite articles of clothing. The next time this happens, you should be prepared to act quickly. Time is the most critical factor in determining whether a stain takes hold or is washed away. You don't have to memorize the following stain removal techniques, but you should be familiar with the main techniques and tools of stain removal.

## Assembling a Stain Removal Kit

Many ordinary household items are useful in removing spots and stains. You probably already have many of these in your home; if you don't they can all be found in your drug, grocery or housewares store. It's a good idea to assemble a spot removal kit that contains one or two items from each of the following categories so that you'll be prepared when the unavoidable spills and stains occur.

Once you've assembled the kit, remember that bleaches, chemicals, and solvents used to remove stains can be caustic or flammable, and some can produce toxic fumes. Be cautious. When working on stains, wear rubber gloves, work in a well-ventilated area, avoid splashing cleaning liquids on your skin or clothing, make sure you don't put your hands near your face or eyes, and don't smoke. Never combine chemicals unless specifically instructed to do so—a strong chemical reaction may do a lot more damage than a stain can. If you want to use one chemical after another, rinse the fabric thoroughly before applying the second chemical.

**Absorbents** (corn meal, fuller's earth, talcum powder, corn starch, powdered chalk): Absorbents, which soak up surface liquids and draw stains out of fabric, are particularly effective on greasy stains. Sprinkle an absorbent liberally over the stained area and leave it there for a few minutes to allow it to become saturated by the liquid. then brush it off and apply a new coat. Repeat until no more liquid is absorbed.

**Detergents:** Since detergents are an easy and useful method of stain removal, keep a powdered laundry detergent and a liquid dishwashing detergent on hand. The liquid detergent must be clear and unscented—perfumes and dyes can hinder stain removal. If a stain removal technique calls for soap, don't use bath soap, which often contains creams, perfumes, or deodorants. Instead, get a powdered or bar laundry soap. You may want to consider an enzyme pre-soak product, which is most effective in treating protein-based stains such as blood, meat juice, or egg. Don't use enzyme pre-soaks on protein-based fibers such as wool or silk.

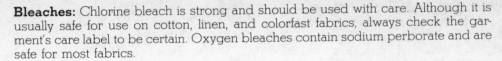

*"Each stain has its own chemical. If someone brings in a dress and points out a stain, the cleaner will spot the stain before cleaning the entire dress. There is no magic solvent that will clean everything."*
— Albert Villenueve

**Bleaches:** Chlorine bleach is strong and should be used with care. Although it is usually safe for use on cotton, linen, and colorfast fabrics, always check the garment's care label to be certain. Oxygen bleaches contain sodium perborate and are safe for most fabrics.

**Chemicals and Acids:** White vinegar, a dilute solution of acetic acid, is effective on many stains. Don't use wine vinegar on stains — you'll probably compound the problem. Dilute white vinegar before you use it on cotton or linen, and avoid using it on acetate. Household ammonia used for stain removal should be clear and unscented. Two other useful stain removing chemicals — oxalic acid, which is used to loosen rust and metallic stains, and sodium thiosulfate, used to treat chlorine discoloration — are available in drug stores.

**Non-Greasy Stain Solvents:** Perchloroethylene, trichloroethylene, trichloroethane, and a variety of naptha (petroleum) mixtures are effective in treating greasy stains. These solvents are also called grease solvents, dry cleaning solvents, cleaning fluids and spot removers, and are found in commercial spot removing preparations. They are available in fluid, paste, and aerosol forms, and your stain removal kit should include at least one.

**Tools and Applicators:** All tools should be cleaned after each use, so you can be sure they're clean the next time you need them. You should have a large ceramic or glass bowl, an old white cotton or terrycloth towel, several sponges, cotton balls, white paper towels, a stainless steel spoon, a soft bristle toothbrush or shoe polish applicator brush, a medicine dropper or syringe, and a pair of rubber gloves.

# Basic Stain Removal Techniques

No matter what caused a stain, there are some general guidelines to follow as you try to remove it.

The first thing you have to do is mop up. Remove any solids in the stain and gently blot liquid left on the fabric surface with paper towels or, even better, by sprinkling an absorbent on the area because the absorbent won't force the stain into the fabric as rubbing with paper towels might. Gently brush the absorbent off before proceeding.

Next, take a moment to identify the fiber content of the material (read the garment's care label), and the staining substance, so that you can choose the right removal treatment. Read all the instructions on the labels of any chemicals, bleaches, or solvents you plan to use. They often include advice and warnings which are important. Because stain removal procedures are presented in general terms, and fabric contents vary tremendously, it is impossible to predict exactly how a specific treatment will affect a particular fabric. Always test *all* treatments you plan to use on an inconspicuous part of the garment such as an inside seam, the back of the hem, an inside pocket, or a shirttail.

Always work on a clean surface, one that is not likely to be affected by either the stain or the chemicals you use to remove it. Glass surfaces, such as the back of a baking dish, plate, platter, or a glass table top are good choices. Whenever possible, turn the fabric inside-out and work from the back to avoid forcing the stain into the material. You can even stretch light-weight fabrics, or those with a loose weave, over a bowl and pour the cleaning solution through the stained area. Heavier fabrics, or those with a dense weave, can be placed on an old towel or cloth while you sponge the treatment into the stain. You should check the towel frequently and reposition the cloth as it becomes soiled.

Keep in mind that the chemicals and techniques used in stain removal can be rather harsh and, if several techniques are offered, always start with the gentlest. If the gentle method doesn't work and you want to try a stronger method, test it first by using small amounts of the cleaning chemical. Don't try to rush the process by using too much. It's better to apply the solution several times than to risk ruining a garment. To avoid leaving a ring after you've removed a stain, always begin treating the outside edges of the stain and work toward the center. Stains which have begun to harden may be softened for easier removal by placing pads soaked in the recommended solution directly above and below the stain and letting them sit for a few minutes. If this doesn't soften and remove the stain, gently roll the fabric between your fingers or, if the fabric is sturdy, rub the stain lightly with the bowl of a spoon.

Always rinse the treated area well after you've removed a stain. Many chemical solutions, diluted in the bottle, become concentrated when their liquid carrying agent evaporates. If traces of concentrated chemicals are left on the fabric, they can cause problems later on. Even laundry detergent can inhibit the action of some performance finishes if they are not rinsed thoroughly. Sponging the affected area with rubbing alcohol will remove any detergent residue, but test the alcohol on the garment first as it can cause some colors to bleed. Always dilute alcohol with two parts water for use on fabrics containing acetate or triacetate fiber.

If the stain is on satin, silk, or other delicate fabrics, blot the liquid and take the garment to a reputable dry cleaner as soon as you can. The dry cleaner is also your best bet if you find yourself unable to remove a stain, if the stain is dried blood, egg or meat juice, if a large area is involved, or if you are unsure of the staining substance.

# The Three General Types of Stains

Most stains fall into one of three general categories: Greasy, non-greasy or a combination of greasy and non-greasy substances. Each has its own treatment method.

## Greasy Stains

To remove stains on washable garments, rub a few drops of liquid detergent into the stain with your fingers. Rinse with water that's as hot as is safe for the fabric. Launder the item as usual. If the stain is still there, place a clean towel beneath the stain and sponge a grease solvent into the area. (Remember to test the solvent on a concealed edge of the garment first.) Grease solvents work just as well after laundering as before. Repeat the solvent application as needed. If the fabric is white it may yellow slightly. If it does, sponge the area with a 50-50 mixture of water and a bleaching agent. Rinse thoroughly. Many finishes tend to hold stains, so be persistent. If the fabric is nonwashable, blot up as much of the liquid as you can with paper towels or an absorbent. Then sponge the stain with grease solvent and let it dry completely. You may have to repeat this procedure several times. If, after several attempts, the stain is still visible and your efforts are no longer removing anything, visit the dry cleaner. Make sure you tell him what the stain is and the cleaning substances that you used on it.

## Non-greasy Stains

For washable fabrics, first sponge the stain with cool water or, if possible, soak the

*"You never know which stains will come out. Some things look impossible and you'll say to the customer 'I'll try, but I doubt it will come out,' yet it comes out beautifully. The next day, someone may bring in exactly the same garment with another stain and it won't come out."*

— Albert Villenueve

entire garment for thirty minutes. Extremely stubborn stains may require overnight soaking. If the spot remains, work a few drops of liquid dishwashing detergent into the stain with your fingers. Rinse thoroughly with warm water. If yellowing or discoloration occurs and the fabric may be bleached, apply a 50-50 solution of bleach and water. Older stains and those which have been ironed in are nearly impossible to remove. For nonwashable fabrics, place an absorbent towel under the stained area and squirt cool water through light fabrics with a medicine dropper or syringe. Sponge heavier materials. If the stain remains, sponge it with a little detergent solution (1 teaspoon liquid detergent to 1 cup water), and rinse by sponging cool water into the area. Rubbing alcohol may be used to remove traces of detergent and aid in drying. However, remember that alcohol can cause colors to bleed and should be diluted with two parts water if the material contains acetate or triacetate. If none of these solvents are successful, take the garment to the dry cleaner and explain the nature of the stain as well as the treatments you applied.

## Combination Stains

When a washable fabric has a stain composed of both greasy and non-greasy substances, treat the non-greasy one first. Lay the stained area on a towel, sponge it with cool water, and use your fingers to work in a few drops of liquid detergent. Rinse with cool water. When the area is dry, sponge the stain with a grease solvent. Repeat as often as necessary. If a trace remains, take the garment to the dry cleaner and explain the source of the stain and how you have treated it.

# A Guide to Specific Stain Treatments

The following chart will help you remove stains caused by specific substances. It will occasionally refer to the cleaning methods described above or to certain solutions. The *detergent solution* is one teaspoon liquid detergent, such as dishwashing detergent, mixed with one cup of warm water. The same basic solution can be obtained by mixing one half teaspoon of powdered laundry detergent with one quart of warm water. An *ammonia and detergent* or *vinegar and detergent solution* is made by adding one tablespoon of ammonia or vinegar to the detergent solution. An *enzyme solution*, unless otherwise noted, refers to a mixture of one tablespoon enzyme pre-soak to one quart water. A *bleach solution* is a mixture of equal parts water and chlorine or sodium perborate bleach. NOTE: Chlorine bleach should not be used when treating silk, wool, spandex, or some fabrics with performance finishes unless specifically mentioned on the garment's care label. Sodium perborate is a peroxygen bleach and many garment care labels specify it as an alternative to chlorine.

**Acids:** Rinse the area immediately and thoroughly with cold water to remove as much of the acid as possible. Sponge with ammonia or a baking soda solution (1 tablespoon of soda to 1 cup of water) to neutralize any remaining acid. Rinse in cold water. Strong acids, such as hydrochloric and sulfuric, can cause severe fiber damage. Weaker acids, such as acetic or citric, probably won't, but they can cause color changes in dyes or fabric finishes. If this happens, the ammonia treatment may restore the color.

**Alcoholic Beverages:** Blot the stain with paper towels and sponge with cold water. If the garment is washable, you can follow the directions for the treatment of a non-greasy stain or you can place a towel under the stain and sponge it with a detergent solution. Rinse and wash as you normally would. An alternative treatment for beer spills on washable fabrics is soaking the garment for thirty minutes in an enzyme solution and then washing normally. If the garment is non-washable, sponge the stain with cold water first, then sponge with a detergent solution. Rinse by sponging with cool water again.

**Alkalies:** Rinse the affected area immediately and thoroughly with cold water. For a strong alkalie, such as lye, place a cloth under the spot and sponge with vinegar to neutralize it. Weaker alkalies, such as ammonia or washing soda, can be washed by a cold water rinse. If the fabric's color has been affected, an application of white vinegar may reverse the damage. Alkalies are most damaging to wool and silk fibers.

**Antiperspirants and Deodorants:** Place the garment on a towel and sponge the stain with warm water. Add a few drops of liquid detergent and work it into the fabric with your fingers. Rinse thoroughly with warm water. Repeat if necessary. As an alternative, combine one teaspoon of bicarbonate of soda and a sprinkle of salt. Add water gradually until a paste forms and apply it to the stained area. Leave it on for fifteen minutes and brush off the residue, then soak the entire garment in an enzyme solution and wash it as you normally would. Some antiperspirants include aluminum salts which may act like acids and discolor the stained area. If this happens, the colors can sometimes be restored by sponging the area with a mixture of equal parts water and ammonia. Nonwashable fabrics should be taken to the dry cleaner.

**Blood:** Soak washable fabrics in cold water until the stain is almost completely gone. Change the water in the basin periodically to keep it clear. Then sponge the stain with a detergent solution and rinse with cold water. (If the stain is stubborn, an ammonia and detergent solution may be necessary.) Wash with warm water and a heavy duty laundry detergent. If you prefer, soak the garment in an enzyme solution before laundering. If traces of the stain remain after laundering, a light application of hydrogen peroxide should remove them. Nonwashable fabrics should be sponged with cold water with a little salt added to prevent colors from bleeding. Sponge with plain cold water to rinse. Blot dry with paper towels. If hydrogen peroxide won't harm the fabric, a mixture of equal parts water and hydrogen peroxide should remove any remaining traces of the stain.

**Butter:** Washable fabrics can be treated with the greasy stain removal method or by sponging the stain with a dry cleaning solvent. Nonwashables should be sponged with a dry cleaning solvent.

**Candle Wax:** If possible, place the garment in the freezer to harden the wax, making it brittle and easy to break off. If this is impractical, use a spoon or dull knife to remove as much wax as possible from the surface. Place the stained area between two paper towels and press with a warm iron. Change the toweling as the wax is absorbed. Any remaining traces may be removed by sponging the area with dry cleaning solvent. If the wax is colored and leaves a tint in the fabric, sponge it with a solution of one part rubbing alcohol and three parts water.

**Candy:** Most candy stains can be removed by using the nongreasy stain removal method. If the candy includes chocolate or a cream syrup use the combination stain removal method.

**Carbon Paper:** Washable fabrics should be sponged with warm water. Work a few drops of liquid detergent into the stain and rinse with warm water. Repeat if needed. If the stain is particularly heavy add a drop or two of ammonia when rubbing in the detergent. Nonwashables will have to be dry cleaned.

**Catsup and Chili Sauce:** Blot the stain with paper towels or by applying an absorbent. Then treat the stain using the nongreasy removal method or by rinsing with cold water and then working a liquid detergent into it with your fingers. If the stain is heavy, add a drop of ammonia when applying the liquid detergent. Launder without rinsing off the detergent. Nonwashables can be treated by sponging in a dry cleaning solvent and allowing it to dry. You may have to repeat this procedure several times.

**Chewing Gum:** If possible, place the garment in the freezer to harden the gum before you attempt to remove it. If that isn't practical, place an ice cube in a plastic bag and rub it against the gum to harden it. Gently work as much gum as possible out of the material. Next, place the stained area on a clean towel and saturate the spot with a grease solvent. You may have to repeat this process several times to remove all the gum. If a sugar stain remains, sponge it with cold water. Nonwashable fabrics may be treated the same way.

**Chlorine:** Resins are applied to a variety of fabrics to provide certain easy care qualities, such as permanent press and wash-and-wear. Some of these resins react with chlorine and cause the finish to yellow or otherwise discolor. Garments made from these fabrics will carry a label warning against the use of chlorine bleach. If you have accidentally bleached such a garment, rinse it immedi-ately in warm water. Soak the rinsed garment in a solution of sodium thiosulfate (1 teaspoon sodium thiosulfate to 1 quart water) and the hottest water safe for the fabric for at least thirty minutes. Rinse completely after treating.

**Chocolate:** Use the combination stain removal method or soak the garment in an enzyme solution for thirty minutes before laundering as usual. Any trace of the stain which remains after treatment may be sponged with a solution of equal parts hydrogen peroxide and water. Rinse with cool water. Sponge nonwashable fabrics with cool water, let dry, and then sponge with a grease solvent. Repeat as necessary.

**Coffee or Tea:** If the beverage contained milk, treat it as a combination stain. If no milk is involved, treat it as a nongreasy stain. Or, you can soak a washable garment in an enzyme solution for thirty minutes. If the stain remains, work a few drops of liquid detergent into the area with your fingers before laundering as usual.

**Cosmetics:** Apply liquid detergent or soap to stains on washable fabrics and rinse with warm water. Repeat as often as needed then launder the item as you normally would.

For stains on nonwashable fabrics, sponge the area with a cleaning solvent and repeat as necessary.

**Crayon:** Crayon stains may be treated the same way you would treat cosmetic stains. If a cleaning solvent does not entirely remove the crayon's color from a nonwashable fabric, take the garment to the dry cleaner.

**Cream:** Sponge stains on washable fabrics with cool water. Work in a few drops of liquid detergent with your fingers and sponge with a detergent solution. Without rinsing, launder as usual. Nonwashable fabrics should be sponged carefully with cool water and then sponged with a grease solvent. When the solvent has evaporated, sponge again with cool water.

**Cream Soups and Sauces:** Washable fabrics may simply require laundering with a heavy duty detergent and warm water. To be safe, treat the stain with a detergent solution before washing. Fabrics which are nonwashable should be sponged with warm water. When dry, sponge in a grease solvent.

**Curry:** Soak washable fabrics in warm water to remove as much of the stain as possible.

Then soak in an enzyme solution before laundering as usual. Nonwashable fabrics should be dry cleaned.

**Dyes:** Always use cold water to avoid setting the dye. Sponge washable fabrics with cold water and then place them in a detergent solution and let them soak for an hour or more. At this point, continue treating as you would a non-greasy stain. Nonwashable fabrics should be taken to the dry cleaners immediately.

**Egg:** Remove any solids left on the surface of the fabric with a dull knife or spoon. Turn the garment inside-out and place it over a towel. Sponge cold water through the fabric. Never use hot water on eggs — it will set the stain. Soak the entire garment in a detergent solution and then launder normally. If the stain is stubborn or heavy you can use an ammonia and detergent solution. Remember to rinse thoroughly. If the stain is on a nonwashable fabric, sponge the area with cold water and let dry. Then carefully sponge in a dry cleaning solvent and let dry.

**Fingernail Polish:** Do not give in to the temptation to apply polish remover. Most contain acetone, which can damage acetate and triacetate fabrics. Sponge amyl acetate

into the stain, removing as much as you can. Then launder the garment as you normally would. If a trace remains after washing, gently dab the area with a cotton ball dampened with alcohol and a drop or two of ammonia. Be sure to test the fabric for alcohol before using this method. For nonwashable fabrics, try sponging with amyl acetate. If the stain is deep or stubborn, take the garment to the dry cleaner as soon as you can.

**Fruit:** Sponge fruit stains with cool water before they dry. If the stain has already dried, dab the area with white vinegar before proceeding. Soak the garment in an enzyme solution and launder as usual. If you don't have an enzyme pre-soak product, follow the directions for removing a non-greasy stain. If traces of the stain remain, apply hydrogen peroxide with a medicine dropper, then rinse thoroughly. Stains on nonwashble fabrics should be sponged with cool water and then with a mild detergent solution, provided this is safe for the fabric. If the detergent solution can't be used, dab the spot with vinegar and rinse by sponging with cool water.

**Furniture Polish:** Use the greasy stain method. If the polish contains wood stain, see PAINTS.

**Glues:** Most airplane and household glues can be removed by sponging the area with acetone or amyl acetate. Use amyl acetate if the fabric contains acetate, triacetate, dynel or verel fiber, all of which can be damaged by acetone. Casein-based adhesives will yield to the non-greasy removal method. Rubber cement can be removed by first rubbing off any cement left on the surface and then sponging the stain with a dry cleaning solvent. Plastic glues can be difficult or impossible to remove unless you catch them before they dry. Work the affected area with a bar of soap and the hottest water that's safe for the fabric. Epoxy cement is impossible to remove. Many other glues and mucilages will come out if you follow the non-greasy stain method with hot rather than the usual cool water.

**Grass, Flowers, Foliage:** Work a liquid detergent into the stain with your fingers then sponge with a detergent solution and rinse well. Sponging with rubbing alcohol will remove most stains of this type from either washable or nonwashable fabrics, but remember to test the alcohol on the fabric first and to dilute it with two parts water if treating acetate or triacetate. Repeat either treatment as often as is needed to remove the stain. If any remains, and it is safe for the fabric, you can sponge the area with hydrogen peroxide. Rinse well with warm water. If the alcohol treatment can't be used on your nonwashables, take the garment to the dry cleaner.

**Gravy:** After blotting the liquid with an absorbent or paper towels, soak washable fabrics in cold water to dissolve the starch. Then treat the stain by sponging with a detergent solution and washing as usual. If the spot is still visible, sponge it with a grease solvent. Repeat as needed. Treat nonwashables by sponging the stain with dry cleaning solvent.

**Grease and Oil:** These types of stains must be treated quickly. If the stain is a heavy grease or road oil, see TAR. All other should be treated using the greasy stain method. If the stain includes dirt and grime it may help to smear the area with vaseline before applying the solvent. Treat nonwashable and sheer fabrics by spreading an absorbent over the stain and allowing it to soak up as much material as possible. As the absorbent becomes gummy, brush it from the fabric. Add fresh absorbent until no more oil is absorbed, then sponge the stain with a grease solvent to remove the remaining oil.

**Ice Cream:** Follow the directions for removing combination stains.

**Inks:** To remove ballpoint pen ink from washables, rinse the area with cold, preferably running, water. Sponge it with a detergent solution, blotting frequently with paper towels to avoid spreading the stain. It may help to gently tamp the material with the bristles of a brush or to rub it with the bowl of a spoon. Next, sponge a dry cleaning solvent into the stain and allow to dry. A bleach solution may be used to treat remaining traces, as long as it is safe for the fabric. It's best to take nonwashable fabrics to the dry cleaner immediately. Don't sponge water into an ink stain on a nonwashable fabric as the stain will spread before you can get it to a dry cleaner. India ink requires immediate attention — once it dries, it will be impossible to remove. Place a pad under the stain and force cool water through the fabric with a medicine dropper or syringe. Next, rub liquid detergent into the stain and rinse. Repeat several times. Then soak the entire garment in a solution of 3 tablespoons ammonia to one quart water. If the stain is particularly heavy, sponge it with ammonia before placing it in the solution to soak. Rinse the garment and launder as usual. Treat nonwashables by forcing water through the stain with a medicine dropper or syringe and then sponging the area with an ammonia and water solution. If the ammonia affects the color of the fabric, dab it with water and then white vinegar and rinse carefully. Printer's ink will usually yield to the greasy stain treatment. If the stain is particularly stubborn, sponge it with turpentine or refer to PAINT. Writing inks vary widely in chemical composition and you may need to try more than one treatment. First, try the treatment for non-greasy stains. If the stain remains, sponge the area with warm water and add a couple of drops of liquid detergent and vinegar. Work it into the stain and rinse well. If the fabric can handle bleach, treat any traces by sponging with a bleach solution. Marking inks are usually impossible to remove, but you should try the non-greasy method before giving up completely.

**Lipstick:** See COSMETICS or apply vaseline and follow directions for greasy stain removal.

**Mayonnaise:** Follow the directions for the removal of a combination stain.

**Meat Juice:** If the stain is fresh, try the combination method. If the stain has dried, take the garment to the dry cleaner.

**Medicine:** Medicine and medications are derived from so many substances that it is difficult to offer a single solution. Start by soaking the garment in cold water or sponging cold water into the area of the stain. If the medication is a gummy substance, it may respond when treated as TAR. Medicines with a sugar base, like many cough remedies, will usually be removed when washed with soap and water. Alcohol based medications should be dabbed with rubbing alcohol and then washed as usual. Remember to dilute the alcohol with two parts water if treating acetate or triacetate fabrics. Nonwashables should be taken to the dry cleaner.

**Mercurochrome and Merthiolate:** Treat these stains as quickly as you can as they are impossible to remove when dry. Soak the entire garment overnight in a solution of warm water, detergent and ammonia. *Use four tablespoons of ammonia rather than the one recommended at the start of this section.* Rinse the garment well after soaking. If the stain remains, sponge the fabric with alcohol, making sure to test alcohol on the garment first as it can cause colors to bleed. Always dilute alcohol with two parts water before using on acetate and triacetate. Handle stains on nonwashables by sponging with alcohol,

if the fabric tolerates it. If the stain remains, place a pad soaked in alcohol under and over the affected area. Keep these pads damp until the stain is drawn out of the fabric. If the garment's colors bleed when alcohol is applied, take it to the dry cleaner immediately.

**Metallic Stains:** These are stains which are caused by rubbing against tarnished metal surfaces. Most of these stains dissolve when sponged with white vinegar or lemon juice. If the stain is heavy, sponge it with acetic acid or oxalic acid instead. Never apply bleach to a metallic stain — it can react with the metal and damage the fibers.

**Mildew:** If a washable fabric has a light or fresh mildew stain, normal laundering should remove it. Rinse thoroughly after washing and dry the garment in the sun. If a trace remains, dab the spot with lemon juice and salt or vinegar and salt and wash again. If the fabric will allow, white cottons and linens may be soaked in a mild bleach solution of one tablespoon of bleach to each quart of water. Mildew stains on nonwashable fabrics should be handled by a dry cleaner. Heavy mildew stains usually include fiber damage and will be impossible to remove.

**Milk:** Treat with the non-greasy method.

**Mud:** Allow the mud to dry on both washable and nonwashable fabric and then brush it from the material. If any traces remain, treat washable fabrics with the non-greasy stain removal method. On nonwashable fabrics, carefully sponge the stain with a detergent solution followed by warm water to rinse.

**Mustard:** Place the stain on a flat smooth surface and gently brush or scrape off any dry mustard. Sponge the stain with a dry cleaning solvent. If the fabric is strong enough, tamp it with the bristles of a brush or rub the area with the bowl of a spoon. Blot the stain frequently with paper towels to remove mustard as it comes free of the fabric. Flush with dry cleaning solvent and allow the fabric to dry. Sponge the traces that may remain with hydrogen peroxide, letting it remain in the fabric for five minutes. Then flush the stain with cool water. If the stain is on a nonwashable garment, sponge it with cold water and take to the dry cleaner or dab the spot with dry cleaning solvent and blot with paper towels to remove the mustard as it is washed from the fabric. Repeat the solvent treatment as necessary.

**Newsprint:** Sponge the mark with a warm detergent solution and rinse with cold water.

Then wash the garment as usual. Marks on nonwashables should be sponged with the detergent solution and then sponged with cold water to rinse.

**Oil:** Salad and vegetable oils should be treated with the greasy stain method. Heavier oils, such as engine oil, should be treated according to the directions under GREASE AND OIL.

**Orange Juice:** See FRUIT.

**Paint and Varnish:** These substances should be treated while fresh or they may be impossible to remove. Check the label for a recommended thinner, which will probably be the best thing to use in removing the stain. Remember to test any chemical on an unexposed area of the garment before applying it to the stained area. Start by *carefully* removing any liquid remaining on the surface with paper towels, tissues, or by applying an absorbent. If the stain is an acrylic paint sponge the spot with warm water and work several drops of the detergent into the stain with your fingers. Next, sponge with a detergent solution and rinse with warm water. Repeat this cycle until the spot is removed. Sponging with turpentine may help to loosen a difficult stain. Sponge again with a detergent solution and rinse. Aluminum paints should be sponged with trichloroethylene (a dry cleaning solvent) unless the fabric contains polyester or triacetate, which call for turpentine. While the stain is still damp from the solvent, place the garment in a detergent solution containing the hottest water safe for the fabric and soak overnight. If the paint involved is enamel, rub vaseline over the spot and take the garment to the dry cleaner. Latex paints can be removed by first flushing the area with cool water to wash as much paint away as possible. Then apply liquid detergent to the stain and work it into the fabric with your fingers. Sponge the area with a warm detergent solution and flush once again with cool water. Repeat if necessary. To remove oil-based paints, start by sponging the stain with a detergent solution. Then rinse with warm water and sponge the area with turpentine or mineral spirits. Sponge once again with the detergent solution and rinse with warm water. Repeat until the stain is gone. Sponge varnish with turpentine and then apply several drops of liquid detergent and work it into the spot with your fingers. Sponge with warm water to rinse. Water colors will usually come out during normal laundering, but to be safe sponge these spots with a detergent solution before you wash.

If you face a particularly difficult paint stain, and the fabric is strong enough, you can tamp the area with the bristles of a brush or rub it with the bowl of a spoon once you have applied the recommended solvent. When you have finished, dabbing the area with alcohol will help remove any residual detergent or turpentine. Remember to test the fabric first and to dilute alcohol for use on acetates and triacetates.

While you can attempt to treat nonwashable and delicate washable fabrics at home, it's safer to rub the spot with vaseline and take the garment to your dry cleaner.

**Pencil:** Both black and colored pencil marks will usually come out when rubbed gently with a soft eraser. If this fails to remove the mark, rub a couple of drops of liquid detergent into the spot and sponge with warm water to rinse. If the mark remains, repeat this procedure and add a drop of ammonia. Rinse again with warm water. Nonwashables may be handled the same way if the fabric will tolerate the detergent. If not, try the eraser and take the garment to the dry cleaner.

**Perfume:** When treating a stain on washable fabric, flush the area with cold water and then sponge the spot with a warm detergent solution. Rinse with cold water. If the spot remains you can soak silk, wool and brightly colored fabrics in a solution of two tablespoons hydrogen peroxide to one gallon water. White cotton, linen, or rayon can be soaked in a solution of one tablespoon bleach to one quart water for fifteen minutes. If a trace remains, sponge the area with alcohol. Remember to test the fabric as rubbing alcohol may cause colors to bleed, and dilute with two parts water if fabric includes acetate or triacetate. Nonwashable fabrics should be sponged with cold water and then alcohol, if this is safe for the fabric. If the stain remains, sponge again with alcohol and place an alcohol-soaked pad above and below the spot. Keep the pads damp until the stain disappears.

**Perspiration:** Perspiration may weaken fibers and cause colors to fade if not removed from the fabric. Fresh stains usually come out in the wash. For an older stain, soak the garment in an enzyme solution before laundering. If the garment's color has been affected, sponging a new stain with ammonia or an old stain with white vinegar will usually restore it. Yellow stains may be removed from white fabrics by using chlorine or sodium perborate bleach when laundering. Remember to rinse well. If an odor persists after washing, soak the garment in a solution of salt water (three tablespoons salt to one quart water). Nonwashables should be sponged with a warm water and detergent solution. Rinse by sponging with warm water. If the color has been affected, and the fabric can tolerate it, sponge with ammonia or vinegar.

**Putty:** Place the entire garment in the freezer to harden the putty and make it easier to remove. If this is not possible then gently scrape as much putty from the fabric as you can and sponge it with a warm detergent solution. Follow this by washing the garment in the hottest water that's safe for the fabric. Use the freezer method on nonwashable fabrics and then take to the dry cleaner.

**Rust:** On washable fabrics use ammonium bifluoride solution (1 tablespoon ammonium bifluoride to one cup water). Ammonium bifluoride can be found at your drugstore. Sponge the spot with the solution and then rinse by sponging with warm water. If the stain is light you can try rubbing the spot with lemon juice and salt. Then let the garment sit for one hour before sponging with warm water to rinse. Delicate fabrics may be handled by moistening the stain with lemon juice and then holding the spot in the steam of a boiling kettle for two or three minutes. Another method, one which should be used only on sturdy fabrics that can handle high temperatures, is to stretch the stained area over a bowl of boiling water and then apply a few drops of oxalic acid to the stain. Rinse the area quickly by dipping it in the bowl of water. If using oxalic acid crystals, sprinkle them on the stain and apply very hot water. When using oxalic acid it is very important to rinse the fabric thoroughly as the acid can destroy fabric if allowed to sit. Rust stains on nonwashable fabrics should be taken to the dry cleaner.

**Salad Dressing:** Use the combination stain removal method.

**Sauces:** Use the combination stain removal method.

**Scorch Marks:** For light scorch marks on washable fabrics you can try the non-greasy method or sponge the mark with a detergent solution followed by a warm water rinse. Then sponge with ammonia and rinse again. Repeat this sequence as needed. For marks on nonwashable fabrics, sponge hydrogen peroxide mixed with one or two drops of ammonia. Test the solution on an unexposed seam before treating the stain. Rinse by sponging with cool water. Rubbing woolens with a silver spoon will sometimes remove light scorch marks. If the damaged fabric is wool or silk there is almost no hope of removing the mark.

**Shellac:** Sponge washable fabrics with dry cleaning solvent and tamp with the bristles of a brush or rub the area with the bowl of a stainless steel spoon. Flush again with solvent. Next sponge with alcohol and work the stain again with the brush or spoon. Sponge again with alcohol. If the stain is stubborn, take it to the dry cleaner. Nonwashables should be taken to the dry cleaner as soon as possible.

**Shoe Polish:** As polishes vary in composition you may have to try several of the following methods before the stain yields. First try the treatment described under COSMETICS. If the stain remains, sponge it with alcohol. Test alcohol before using on the stain as it may cause colors to bleed, and dilute it with two parts water for use on acetate and triacetate. Scrape off as much as you can using

a spoon or a dull knife. Then follow the directions for greasy stain removal. If the problem persists, sponge the stain with turpentine and then with a detergent solution followed by warm water. Repeat the turpentine application and launder. With nonwashable fabrics, remove as much of the substance as you can and take the garment to a dry cleaner.

**Tea:** See COFFEE AND TEA.

**Tobacco:** Follow the method for GRASS, FLOWERS AND FOLIAGE.

**Tomato Juice:** Follow the non-greasy stain removal method.

**Varnish:** See PAINT AND VARNISH.

**Vaseline:** Follow the greasy stain method.

**Vegetables:** Follow the non-greasy stain method.

**Vinegar:** If the vinegar has changed the colors in the fabric follow the procedure under ACIDS.

**Wax:** Floor or furniture wax should be handled with the greasy stain method. If the wax is from a candle, see CANDLE WAX.

**Wine:** For red wine stains on washable fabrics blot up as much as you can using paper towel or an absorbent. Sponge the stain with a warm detergent solution and then with cold water to rinse. If the stain is particularly difficult you can make a paste of dry laundry or dishwasher detergent and gently work it into the stain with an old toothbrush. Rinse thoroughly with cold water. Spritzing delicate fabrics with club soda may do the trick. Difficult stains may also be soaked in an enzyme solution before washing. White wine can usually be removed by sponging the area with cool water. If the stain remains, sponge it with a warm detergent solution and then launder as usual. For white wine on nonwashable fabrics, try sponging with club soda. If the stain remains take the garment to the dry cleaner.

# LAUNDRY AND DRY CLEANING

No matter how well you care for your clothes, they won't look their best if they aren't clean. As simple as keeping your clothes clean may seem, there are a few techniques and materials that you should be aware of in order to keep your wardrobe in top condition.

The key to cleaning is the garment's care label. Nearly all garments carry them. The label indicates the fibers contained in the garment, whether or not it has been treated with any finishes to make it permanent press, wash-and-wear, etc., and the best way to clean it. Be aware, however, that the label is not obligated to state that certain fabrics should not be bleached, or that others are likely to shrink when washed — you're expected to know that. (*A Guide to Fabrics*, which begins on page 26, will clear up questions you may have about the characteristics of certain fabrics and finishes.) The most common instructions carried on care labels include:

**Machine Wash:** The garment is sturdy. If the label offers no more specific instructions, you can wash it on the 'regular' cycle, tumble it dry, and bleach it.

**Dry Clean:** The garment may water spot and should be cleaned with special care. It's best to take the item to a dry cleaner, but you may want to try using a self-service dry cleaning machine.

**Professionally Dry Clean Only:** Don't try doing it yourself; take it to an expert.

**No Chlorine Bleach:** But a gentler, oxygen bleach may be used.

**Cold, Warm,** or **Hot Wash:** Tells you where to set the water temperature dial on the washing machine.

**Delicate** or **Gentle Cycle:** Set the dial on the washing machine for one of these less vigorous cycles.

**Durable** or **Permanent Press Cycle:** Either of these cycles will give the garment a warm water wash, short spin, and a cool rinse. If your machine doesn't offer these settings, set it for 'normal' with a warm water temperature.

**Wash Separately:** The colors in the item are likely to run or bleed so it should be washed alone or with other garments that are similar in color.

**Hand Wash:** The garment is fairly fragile and should be washed by hand with lukewarm water and a mild detergent. If you prefer, it may be dry cleaned.

**Hand Wash Separately:** The garment may bleed and should be washed by hand alone or with similar colors.

### To Avoid Shrinkage

Buy clothes labeled 'pre-shrunk,' or 'sanforized,' and then follow the garment's care label instructions. Because the heat and agitation of machine washing allow yarns to soften and lose their shape, use cold water and a gentle agitation on those items you want to protect. Don't let them get heavily soiled — cold water doesn't clean as well as hot.

**Tumble Dry, Low, Medium**, or **High:** The garment may be machine dried at the setting indicated.

**Remove Promptly:** The garment is probably permanent press and should be taken from the dryer as soon as the cycle is finished to minimize wrinkling.

**Drip** or **Line Dry:** Don't use the dryer. Hang the item on a wooden hanger or a clothesline and let it dry naturally.

**Dry Flat:** Commonly found on knitted items. The garment should be placed on a flat surface (over a towel), reshaped, and allowed to dry naturally. You can speed the drying time by gently rolling the garment in a towel first to blot excess moisture.

**Cool, Medium,** or **Hot Iron:** Tells you what ironing temperature the fabric can tolerate.

# Sorting

Before you toss your clothes into the washing machine, they need to be sorted. After checking the labels, divide your clothes into machine washables, hand washables, and dry cleanables. First, concentrate on machine washables. Sort this pile into three smaller piles — one for dark or brightly colored items, one for light colored items, and one for whites. As you sort, pull pockets inside-out to empty them and ensure that they'll be washed, too. Fasten buttons, zippers, hooks-and-eyes and other clasps to keep them from catching and possibly ripping other garments during the wash. Some items, like corduroy trousers and washable sweaters, should also be turned inside-out to keep them from picking up lint or pilling. Remove pins and other non-washable decorations from clothes before washing.

# Laundry Aids

Water is an often ignored but extremely important part of effective laundering. Hard water — with a high concentration of chemicals and minerals — inhibits the cleaning action of soaps and detergents so the clothes aren't being soaped and rinsed properly and may appear dingy. The easiest solution to the problem is to use a water conditioning product at the beginning of the wash cycle. It will keep the minerals in suspension and let them be rinsed away.

Soaps and detergents are the cleaning agents you'll usually use. Soaps, which contain alkalies and fats, are most effective in soft water. Detergents, synthesized from petroleum and animal or vegetable by-products, can be used in hard or soft water. Both work in the same way — they loosen the soil from your clothes, break it down into tiny particles, and then surround it so that it isn't redeposited on the fabric.

Bleaches help to brighten white and colorfast fabrics. Because some fabrics react badly to bleach, it's particularly important to read a garment's care label before bleaching. Liquid chlorine bleach, the strongest and least expensive variety, is not suitable for all fabrics and finishes. Never use it on wool, silk, spandex, acetate, or any permanent press fabric unless the label specifically calls for it. As an alternative you can use an oxygen bleach, which isn't quite as strong as chlorine bleach and is safe for most finishes, fibers, and colorfast fabrics.

Never pour bleach on dry clothes. Add it to the washing machine after the machine has been filled with water so that the bleach will be diluted before you add clothes. And don't use bleach every time you wash — every fourth or fifth time should be enough to keep fabrics bright.

**Enzyme pre-soaks** can help loosen heavy soil before clothing is washed. The action of the enzymes is particularly useful in treating protein-based stains like blood, meat juice, or egg. They should not, however, be used on protein-based fibers such as wool or soil. Soiled garments can simply be soaked in the solution (don't mix light and dark fabrics) and then laundered as usual.

**Disinfectants** can kill organisms that would otherwise survive for weeks on the inner surfaces of a washing machine. Bacteria, fungi, and viruses won't be destroyed by even the hottest water a washing machine has available, so you may want to add a disinfectant to the wash cycle, especially if you're using a public laundromat. Simply follow the label directions. Bleaches also serve as mild disinfectants.

Fabric softeners, available as liquids, sprays, sheets, or solids are used in the washing machine or the dryer to reduce static cling, soften fabric, reduce wrinkling, and cut down on lint. While fabric softeners are a big help, they can also cause temporary greasy spots if used improperly, so always follow label directions. One caution: Fabric softener can reduce a fabric's absorbency so don't use it every time you wash towels or other items that should remain absorbent — every third or fourth time should be enough.

## Machine Washing

Using a washing machine is easy. It's just a matter of choosing the proper water

*"It's best to wash jeans inside-out to keep the dye from coming out of them. And they'll fade even less if you wash them by hand."*
— Frank Hurd

temperature, water level, and cycle for the items you're washing. If you own a washing machine, read the owner's manual for valuable information about the best way to use your machine.

**Water Temperature:** As a rule, hot water (130°-150° F/54°-65° C) is reserved for whites, light colored cottons, linen, and heavily soiled permanent press or drip dry fabrics. Warm water (100°-110° F/38°-43° C) is best for dark colorfast fabrics, permanent press fabrics, some washable woolens (check the label), and most synthetics. Rinse in cool water, if possible. Cold water (80°-100° F/27°-37° C) is for non-colorfast clothing, some washable woolens (check the label), bright colors, and delicate items.

Fabrics made from fiber blends should be washed according to the procedures for the predominant fiber in the blend. If you're not sure what that is, it's safest to choose a cool temperature and mild cycle.

**Water Level:** Set the water level so that the clothes will be covered by about half an inch of water. This allows them to circulate freely and get clean without wasting water.

**Cycle:** Although machines differ from manufacturer to manufacturer, most have a normal cycle and a gentle cycle and many have a special setting for permanent press items. Each cycle includes a wash, rinse, and spin dry. When you select a cycle, you are determining how long your clothes will be agitated and how vigorous the agitation will be. Generally, sturdy white or colorfast items should go in the normal cycle for 10 to 12 minutes; sturdy garments which may bleed can go in the normal

### General Tips to Prevent Shrinkage

**1.** Wash an item before it gets heavily soiled — this lets you use a milder detergent, gentle agitation, and cooler water temperature.
**2.** Use the gentle cycle if the garment is lightly soiled.
**3.** Wash blended fabrics in warm water and use a cool rinse.
**4.** When machine drying, use a low temperature setting and remove dress shirts while damp.
**5.** Drip or line dry whenever possible.

cycle for 6 to 8 minutes. Permanent press, wash-and-wear, and other easy care fabrics should go in the permanent press cycle, which includes a cool rinse and a short spin. If a special permanent press cycle isn't available, use the normal cycle for 6 to 8 minutes and set the machine for a warm wash with a cool rinse. Delicate fabrics, like washable woolens, knits, and lingerie should be set at gentle for 2 to 6 minutes.

After you've chosen a cycle, fill the basin with water and add the soap or detergent, which should be dissolved before you add the clothes. Don't stuff the machine with clothes — they should be able to circulate freely.

## Washing by Hand

Hand washables should be laundered separately, but if you have quite a few items to wash break them down into light and dark colors and do two loads. Fill a sink or washtub halfway with cool or lukewarm water and add a mild detergent. Stir the solution with your hand to make sure the detergent dissolves completely. Submerge the clothes and let them soak for 3 to 5 minutes, then gently squeeze (never wring or rub) the solution through the fabric, which should remain immersed. After squeezing each item for 3 to 5 minutes, rinse well in cool water. Rinse two or three times to make sure that you have removed all of the detergent and soil. When lifting delicate items from water, support the entire garment to avoid pulling and stretching it. Blouses, dresses, scarves, and lingerie can be dried by draping them over the shower rod in the bathtub. If you use hangers instead, make sure that they are wood. Wire hangers will stretch and mark wet fabrics. Sweaters, stockings, and lingerie may be rolled in a towel to blot excess moisture before drying. Sweaters and other knits should always be dried on a flat surface, away from direct sunlight or heat.

**To Counteract Shrinkage**

Before washing woolens or knits, place the garment on a sheet of plain brown wrapping paper and outline it in pencil. After laundering, while the material is damp, lay the garment on the pattern and gently stretch it back into shape. Pin it to the paper until it's dry.

# Drying Clothes

Almost all clothes, except woolens and knits, can be dried on a clothesline or a wooden hanger. Woolens and knits should be rolled in a towel to remove excess moisture, then placed on a towel on a flat surface, reshaped, and allowed to dry naturally.

Before hanging clothes out to dry, make sure that the clothespins and clothesline are clean. Wash the pins in a mild detergent, and wipe the line with a damp sponge. Hang white and light colored fabrics in the sun — its natural bleaching effect will keep them bright. Colors and delicate items should be hung away from direct sunlight. Always hang garments by their sturdiest points, usually at a seam, to keep them from stretching under the added weight of moisture. As you hang clothes, smooth fabric, straighten collars, open sleeves, and run your fingers along the seams to minimize the need for ironing later. Items which do need ironing should be ironed while still damp.

Machine drying is easy, and there are a couple of techniques that can make it especially effective. Shake each garment before placing it in the dryer to reduce the wrinkles caused by washing. If you're drying a load of mixed fabrics, stop the cycle periodically to remove dry items. Remove permanent press items as soon as the cycle ends and hang them up to minimize the need for ironing.

Never machine dry woolens unless the label says you can, and even then use a low temperature and a short cycle. If you're in doubt about the best way to dry a particular garment, set the machine on a low temperature and check it frequently during the cycle.

**Sending it Out:** If doing your own laundry requires too much time or trouble, there

*"To get them really clean, I always boil all my white T-shirts. It doesn't shrink them, and it takes all the stains out. I let them simmer for about 20 minutes and then I take them out and rinse them two or three times in tepid water."*
—Frank Hurd

are several options you can choose from. Bear in mind that it's best to use a commercial laundry that does its work on the premises. Large central plants use very hot water for washing, very high drying temperatures, and industrial strength detergents, three factors that can cause your clothes to deteriorate quickly. There's also the risk of having your clothes misplaced. You're far better off to choose among one of these three options:

**Hand Laundries:** This is the best, but most expensive, choice. Your clothes are treated gently and carefully.

**Chinese Laundries:** This is also an excellent choice. Chinese laundries are noted for gentle detergents and courteous service.

**Coin-Operated Laundry:** The least expensive, but hardest on your clothes. You will be charged by the pound for washing and folding clothes; by the item for ironing.

On your first visit to any laundry, ask about the methods they use and the services they offer. If you want an item handled in a specific fashion, make sure you tell them. If, after two or three visits, you aren't satisfied with the service, try another.

## Dry Cleaning

There are two dry cleaning options — a coin-operated dry cleaning machine, or a professional dry cleaner. However, it's wisest to see a professional dry cleaner who can give your clothes the individual attention they require.

When gathering clothes to take to the cleaner, take a moment to inspect them for missing buttons, spots, stains and tears that you should tell the dry cleaner about. To ensure that your clothes come back spotless, you have to tell the cleaner what caused specific stains so that he can use the appropriate treatment. Don't wait to have stained garments cleaned — there's a far better chance of removing fresh stains than there is of removing ones that have set.

Choose a dry cleaner that does work on the premises rather than sending items to a central plant — you'll probably get faster, more attentive service and you'll definitely reduce the risk of lost garments.

When you pick up your dry cleaning, look at the clothes carefully. If they are not cleaned to your satisfaction, discuss it with the owner. If a garment needs additional cleaning, the dry cleaner should be willing to do it at no charge. Check to make sure that creases are smooth and sharp, and that lapels are smooth and not pressed flat against the jacket. The best dry cleaners pay attention to minor details, such as attaching loose buttons and stuffing sleeves with tissue paper to help them keep their shape, without being asked.

*"In India I did all my lady's dry cleaning with petrol. I once washed one of her dresses and the dye ran. The only way to get it out was to wash each piece of the dress separately, because if you wash a dress that is sewn the double material on the seam can run. I unpicked all the dress and washed each piece separately and very carefully and then, with the aid of an Indian servant, I sewed up the long evening dress and all the different pieces. When it was finished I brought it to my lady and all she said was, 'That was an experience, wasn't it?'"*

— Mlle. Elise Gaubert

# IRONING AND PRESSING

Ironing puts the finishing touch on freshly laundered clothes and a crisp look back into crumpled garments. But it is a double-edged weapon—the more you iron, the more you have to iron. And too much ironing wears out fabric. Using a cloth and iron together is known as 'pressing,' putting the iron directly onto the fabric is called ironing. If you continually freshen up unlaundered clothes by ironing or pressing them, you'll seal in the odors and eventually seal in the wear marks. To avoid this, don't iron or press clothes too often and don't put the iron directly onto the right side of most fabrics. This also prevents putting a shine on the material—a shine that indicates age and wear. As a general rule, iron light-weight fabrics on the wrong side and press heavier fabrics and light-weight suitings through a clean cloth on the right side. The cloth you use should be a finished cotton towel that won't leave fluff behind, such as a linen tea towel.

## Irons

Before the days of electric irons, people used crudely shaped 'flat irons' that weighed up to six or seven pounds and were heated on a stove. Heavier fabrics needed heavier irons, and in large country houses with billiard tables a 15 lb. iron was used to keep baize smooth.

An iron's weight no longer determines the weight of the fabric it can iron, but it should feel comfortable and balanced in your hand. More importantly, when choosing an iron, bear in mind what you are going to use it for. A traveling dry iron may be ideal for popping into a suitcase but it's too small for everyday use. And, although most clothes should be ironed damp, many professionals are against using a steam iron. They say it can leave wet patches that will turn into watermarks on silks and cottons.

**Dry Irons:** Have a heat-selecting dial which is controlled by a thermostat. These light-weight irons have a slim, pointed soleplate and a low body to make intricate ironing easier.

**Steam Irons:** A dry iron which can also supply steam through holes or grooves in the soleplate. There is only one setting for steam and it can easily be switched back to dry ironing. Steam will cease when the iron is stood on its heel.

**Steamers:** These make ideal traveling irons. They are much lighter to use than conventional steam irons, and as they maintain a constant flow of hot steam, they are less likely to leave wet patches on the material. They steam away wrinkles on delicate fabrics with no risk of scorching. They are excellent for smoothing silk and velvet and for de-wrinkling neckties while they are hanging on a hanger or rail. You can also use them for smoothing jackets, skirts and dresses while the garments are still hanging

*"Remember that pressing is like dry cleaning — you are causing wear every time you do it. Only press a garment when it needs it. The back of a trouser leg always need pressing because it always creases, so you can just press that a bit. If the front leg crease has dropped out, then put that back in without doing the rest of the trousers."*

— Mark Fairweather

on their hanger. Most models include a brush and an ironing sleeve for dry ironing.

**Use:** After you have filled your steamer with water as directed, turn it on and stand it on its end to wait for the steam to appear, about one minute. You can then point the steamer up toward a hanging garment. Never point it down — it will leak. The steamer can be used horizontally as long as you wipe the steam outlet to ensure against leaving drops of water on the fabric.

The garment must be bone dry before you begin. Then slowly smooth out the wrinkles with the steamer. There is no need to press down heavily onto the fabric — go over it lightly and let the steam do all the work. When not in use, stand the steamer on its end.

**Ironing Temperatures:** It doesn't matter how hot an iron is if you are using a cloth to protect the fabric. When ironing, iron on the wrong side and follow the care instructions on the label in your garment. Modern irons have three temperature settings:
**Hot** (210°C/410°F) Cotton, linen, rayon (viscose) or modified rayon (modal);
**Warm** (160°C/320°F) Polyesters, mixtures, wool;
**Cool** (120°C/248°F) Acrylic, nylon, acetate, triacetate, polyester.

**Starch:** Spray starch is popular and easy to use. After spraying it on, let it soak in for a few seconds before you start ironing, so that the material can absorb the starch and starchy flakes won't stick to the soleplate of the iron.

**Maintenance:** A good iron will last 10 years or so if you treat it right. Stand and store it on the heel rest, and if it's a steam iron, use distilled water to fill the tank (hard water clogs it up). Empty it out when the iron is still warm.

You can clean starch or brown marks from the face of an iron by rubbing it with a damp piece of coarse cloth held taut over the edge of an ironing board.

For stubborn marks, rub gently with fine steel (wire) wool. When cleaning a steam iron, hold it horizontally in the ironing position so that nothing becomes lodged in the steam vents.

## Ironing Boards

A wooden table works as well as an ironing board. The wood should be covered with a folded blanket to cushion the iron and absorb the moisture from the steam. Cover the blanket with a sheet to protect the garment from fluff. Use a sleeve board for a smooth finish on blouse and dress sleeves. According to lady's maid Mademoiselle Elise Gaubert, lady's maids would never dream of ironing sleeves on their ladies' dresses without using a sleeve board. When maids traveled with their employers, they took special sleeve boards with them. These boards were small enough to pop in a suitcase and were made out of cardboard, padded with flannel, and slip-covered with cotton.

# Fabrics

**Wool and Tweed:** Brush wool and heavy suitings before pressing them with a hot iron and damp cloth. The iron should be as hot as possible to generate the maximum amount of steam, as this opens up the strong fibers and smooths away creases.

**Duties of the Lady's Maid**

Her first duty in the morning...is to examine the clothes put off by her mistress the evening before, either to put them away, or to see that they are all in order to put on again...the lady's maid should prepare for dressing her mistress, arranging her dressing-room, toilet table, and linen...Ironing is a part of the duties of a lady's maid, and she should be able to do it in the most perfect manner when it becomes necessary.

—Mrs. Beeton's Book of Household Management, 1861

To dampen the cloth, wet it thoroughly and then wring it out very firmly so that it is fairly dry. Or, if you prefer, you can spray the cloth with a fine stream of water as you press. Use a spray mister, the type used for watering plants. Always keep the iron moving, and when you have finished an area make sure the steam has stopped rising from the iron before you continue.

**Acrylic:** Iron dry with a cool iron.

**Velvet:** You can steam the garment on a hanger with a steamer, or hold it near a boiling kettle, or an iron wrapped in a damp cloth to generate steam. A lot of people hang velvet in the bathroom while they have a hot bath or shower. But if you do that, be careful not to do what a friend did when staying in a grand country house in England. She hung her evening dress on the shower rail and had a bath. As she got out, her dress fell in.

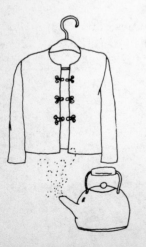

**Cottons, Linens, and Silks:** You can use a steamer on silk. If you don't have one, spray silks, cottons or linens with a spray mister and then roll them up in large bath towel to absorb all the moisture. The garment should still be slightly damp when you unwrap it. Cotton and linen should be left rolled in the towel for about half an hour, but silk needs more time. A silk shirt should be left for at least three hours, and a silk dress from four to 24 hours, as long as it doesn't become bone dry. You will usually find that a warm iron (160° C/320° F) on silk is sufficient to remove creases. Use a hot iron (210° C/410° F) on cotton and linen. The finish on wild silk is less smooth than on ordinary silk and it should be ironed dry. Do not roll up suits. Instead, iron them on the wrong side while they're damp, or press them on the right side with a hot iron and damp cloth.

**Lingerie:** Use a steamer or iron the damp garment on the wrong side at a moderate temperature. If the iron is too hot the material will stick to the soleplate; if it's too cool it won't remove all the wrinkles.

**Drip Dry Fabrics:** You can press lightly on the wrong side with a cool iron, but since the creases should fall out if the garment has been hung correctly, and they will invariably fall out from the heat of your body, ironing really isn't necessary

# To Press Suits

**Jackets:** Footman Mark Fairweather always brushes a jacket before he presses it, and he only presses a jacket when he has to. "A jacket usually creases on the inside of the elbow and at the back," he says, "and these areas can be pressed without doing the rest of the jacket." But when it's absolutely necessary, he brushes a jacket as follows.

**Waistcoat:** Although the lining at the back creases very easily, it only takes a couple of minutes to press.

*"You should never press hard on a seam; and always iron underneath a seam after you have ironed it flat to get rid of the seam mark."*
— Mlle. Odile Barbiere

**Trousers:** A crisp looking front crease is essential, and it was once the yardstick that valets used to judge how well a gentleman was looked after. For a sharp crease the pants must be pressed, and as brushing and pressing go hand-in-hand, always brush the trousers first. To locate the correct positioning of the creases, pick the pants up by the cuffs and line up the four seams. The front and back creases on

(continued on page 135)

## How Mark Fairweather Irons a Jacket

**1.** Unbutton the jacket and lay it flat with the lining face down on a table. Fold out the lapels so that they lie flat, and use a hot iron and damp cloth to press them from where they start above the buttons and buttonholes to where they end, just beyond the V where they join the collar. Never press the collar itself as you want it to roll over naturally, not have a knife-edge crease.

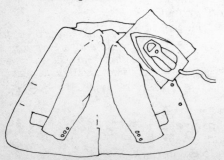

**2.** Next iron the back. Turn the jacket over so that the lining is face up. Iron directly onto the lining. If the lining is silk, squirt water directly on it with a plant spray mister and use a warm iron (160° C/320° F) or a high wool setting. Push the vents to one side to iron the back flap. (The back gets crumpled from sitting, but the vents don't wrinkle so easily. However, you can iron them if they need it.)

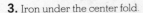

**3.** Iron under the center fold.

**8.** For a professional finish, hang the jacket where you can reach around it easily. A steamer gives the best results, but a damp cloth wrapped around an iron works nearly as well. Start with the cuffs. Put a clothes brush inside the first cuff (bristles facing outward) and just touch the creases with the steamer or cloth-wrapped iron. Then lightly touch up the front of the jacket.

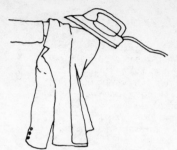

**4.** Fold in the sides and lay the first sleeve flat. Use a hot iron and a damp cloth. As steam penetrates both sides of the sleeve, press the inside so as not to cause more wear on the outside.

**5.** Press the second sleeve.

**6.** Iron the shoulders when you have finished both sleeves. Turn the first shoulder inside-out and hold a clothes brush so that the material lies over the bristles and the handle presses into the palm of your hand. Use a spray mister to dampen the lining, then iron directly on it.

**7.** Iron the second shoulder.

### How to Iron Trousers

**1.** Fold the top leg back from the leg underneath and pull back the pockets. If the trousers are lined make sure the lining is flat. Smooth the bottom leg and start with the front crease. Lay a dry cloth over it and dampen it with a spray mister. As you work the hot iron down the crease, pull the cloth back to make sure that you are not accidentally creating more creases. Press the crease from the waistband to the cuffs by spraying the cloth, placing the iron over the damp patch and sliding it back and forth three or four times on the same area until the steam has completely disappeared. Then move the iron down the crease and repeat.

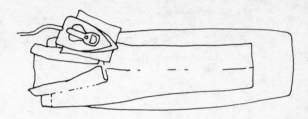

**2.** Press the rest of the leg, the back crease, and around the crotch. Pull back the first leg and press the second leg underneath. There's usually no need to press the waistband, but if you want to, it's easiest to finish off by pressing it on a sleeveboard.

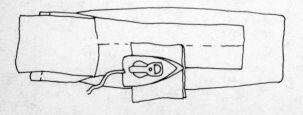

## How to Iron a Waistcoat

**1.** Lay the waistcoat face up to iron the back of the lining. Use a spray mister to lightly dampen it, then iron directly on the lining with a warm iron (160° C/320° F) or at a high wool setting.

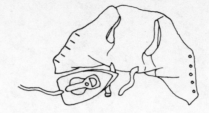

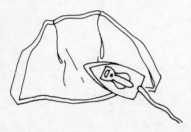

**2.** Turn the waistcoat over to iron the buckle strap. Lay the buckle strap flat and press the inside.

**3.** Press the outer fabric of the vest with a hot iron (210° C/410° F) over a damp cloth. Make sure you bring the iron up to the edge of the buttons and give that area a quick press, too.

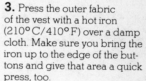

## How to Iron a Skirt

Use an ironing board so that you can turn the skirt around as you iron or press it. Start by turning it inside-out.

**1.** Lay the skirt on the board and iron the facings, seams, and pockets. Iron under the seams to avoid a mark.

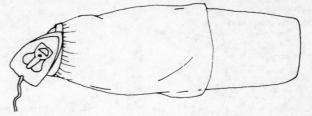

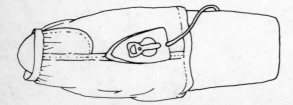

**2.** If you want to press on the right side using a damp cloth, start by pressing the waistband. Then, press the back, the front, and the sides. Avoid pressing the pockets, which may leave an outline on the skirt.

each leg should fall midway between them. Lay the trousers on the ironing surface with the front creases nearest you. You need only iron the inseam of each leg, as the warmth and steam go right through both sides. Don't iron both legs together as the top leg will mark the one underneath.

**Pleats:** The crispest pleats are tacked before they're pressed. Sew under the pleats and run your tacking stitches about an inch from the bottom of the skirt. Press on the right side with a damp cloth.

**Shirts and Blouses:** It's usually safe to iron directly on either side of the fabric. Unbutton the shirt and lay it face up with the collar turned out. Start with the collar and work from its points to the center back. Then turn the shirt over to iron behind the buttonholes, buttons, collar, and yoke. Iron the shoulders by putting them over the end of the ironing board.

Iron inside and outside the cuffs before ironing both sides of the sleeves. Run the iron along the underseams first and then iron from the tops of the sleeves down into the gathers at the cuff and up again toward the shoulder, where the crease is on most shirts. But you may choose the royal distinction of the crease sported by the Prince of Wales and the Duke of Edinburgh—one that falls on the inside of the sleeve rather than at the top.

Ladies' blouses often look better without any sleeve crease at all, a look that is achieved by putting the ironing pad of the sleeve board inside the sleeve.

Iron the body of the shirt last. Start at the back, then iron the front. Finish off by turning down the collar and pressing it. Fold an ironed shirt as described on page 60.

# How to Iron Frills

The secret of making frills stand up crisply is to iron directly on the gathers. Iron frills before anything else. Lay them flat on the ironing board. Hold the iron in one hand and steady the shirt with the other. Place the iron directly on the gathers of the frill, then slowly draw it away. Turn the shirt so that you iron every detail. Iron underneath the frill before you iron the rest of the shirt. When you've finished ironing the garment, touch up the frills once more.

**Lace:** The trick to ironing lacy details is to cushion the lace on a soft pad covered with a clean cloth. Lightly press the back of the lace with a damp cloth and warm iron until the pattern stands out sharply. As with frills, it's easiest to start by ironing lacy details and then to touch them up again before you put the garment away.

# Dresses, Jeans, Sweaters and Ties

**Dresses:** The general rules for ironing a dress are the same as for ironing a skirt and shirt. Turn the dress inside-out and iron the interfacings, the lining, and behind the buttons and buttonholes. Iron both sides of the collar. Continue ironing silk and delicate fabrics on the wrong side, or iron through a dry cloth on the right side.

Iron the yoke and the shoulders. Iron inside and outside the cuffs before doing the sleeves. When that's done, turn the dress on the board and, ironing downward, iron the back and front of the bodice.

Always iron the bodice before ironing the skirt. Start at the back of the skirt and turn it around the board, ironing from the waist to the hem. If the dress has ties,

*"Never fold material while it is still damp or it will crease. By the time you have finished ironing, the item must be bone dry."*
— Mlle Odile Barbiere

iron them last.

**Jeans:** Take them out of the dryer when they are slightly damp and press them on the wrong side using a very hot iron. Lay them flat and follow the ironing instructions for other trousers (see page 129), but iron both sides of the leg. Then, turn the jeans right side out and brush each leg from the waistband to the cuff to soften the material.

**Sweaters:** Use a warm iron over a damp cloth, as a hot iron can matt wool, making its fibers stiff and hard. Press lightly, working downward. Press the back and then turn over the sweater to press the front. Work on the sleeves last. To remove an elbow or hanger mark, press it lightly and then gently knead the wool with your fingertips. Repeat until the mark disappears.

**Ties:** There's no need to iron a knitted or tweed tie if it's been washed and dried properly. Because silk ties become shiny if pressed or ironed, you should use a steamer or wrap a damp cloth around an iron and stand it on its end. Hold the tie above and in front of it in one hand. Have a clothes brush in the other hand, and as the steam rises from the cloth, release the tie so that each part of it rests on the steamy cloth. Brush out the wrinkles as the tie slides over the cloth.

# EMERGENCY REPAIRS

"Hems come down, zippers stick, buttons pop off, and petticoats have been known to fall down in the middle of the stage," says Maureen Gavin, wardrobe mistress to the British Royal Ballet Company's ballerinas since 1973. "Sometimes the elastic straps that hold up a dancer's tutu break. We usually check that the elastic on all the tutus is secure, but it's easy to overlook one. Then it becomes very embarrassing. The dancer has her arms up in the air, the strap 'pings,' and her boobs fall out."

The key to dealing with emergencies is to repair the problem right away, either by doing it yourself or having it done professionally. Remember that a 'stitch in time' can save a favorite garment.

**Professional Repairs:** If you're not an expert with a needle and thread, leave the big jobs — taking seams in or out, putting in zippers, hemming skirts and trousers — to a repair specialist. Before you leave a garment for repairs, ask a few questions. If the repair will cost more than half what the garment cost new, or if you don't plan on wearing the item through at least one more season, then it's probably not worth having it repaired. If you do want the garment fixed, remember that there's no such thing as a completely invisible repair.

"Invisible mending only works on woven fabrics such as tweed," notes Sava Rasic Harris, owner and operator of *Mark of Knightsbridge*, one of London's finest dry cleaning and repair specialists. "Most mending, however well done, will show, but a good repair is one that shows as little as possible."

**Doing It Yourself:** Doing minor repairs yourself can be relaxing and economical, but don't even attempt it when you don't have the time to do it properly. "People sometimes come to us with a repair that they have done themselves," says Albert Villeneuve, who has been with the highly regarded *Guillaume*, dry cleaning and tailoring specialists in London for 50 years. "They want us to improve it because they did it in a hurry and it looks much worse than it would if they had left it alone. The golden rules are 'don't make a repair in a hurry unless you absolutely have to, and make sure you work in a light that's strong enough to let you see what you're doing.'"

**Zippers, Buttons and Fasteners:** Maureen Gavin of the Royal Ballet is an expert on instant repairs. "About 20 zippers are worn in different costumes during each performance, so at least one is going to go. It happens all the time," she says. "But we can easily mend a zipper to last the duration of the performance. In fact, it could last two or three performances, but we always replace faulty zippers as soon as we can."

**Buttons:** The button box in your sewing kit allows you to keep stray buttons together until you have time to sew them on. In addition to the button, you'll need a one and one half inch long needle with a medium-sized eye and thread that closely

## Royal Ballet Quick Zipper Repair

**1.** Make a horizontal cut above the missing tooth on the side opposite the slider.

**2.** Hook the slider up into the teeth above the missing teeth, so that it engages both sides, and pull the slider to the top of the zipper.

**3.** To sew the open portion of the zipper closed, begin on the tooth above the horizontal cut and, using double thread, work six or seven small, even stitches from side to side, firmly bringing the fabric tapes of the zipper together.

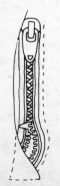

**4.** Sew four or five rows of stitches across the open teeth down to the bottom of the zipper.

matches the color of the garment or the thread that's on the other buttons. Use extra-strong thread to replace buttons on heavy garments such as jackets and coats. You can reinforce buttons by anchoring them to a smaller button sewn into the inside of the garment.

After the needle is threaded (a needle threader can make this easier), knot the loose ends of thread together. Position the button on the garment and, starting on the wrong side of the fabric, push the needle through a hole in the button. Be careful not to pull the thread too tight—you should leave about an eighth of an inch between the button and material. Push the needle back through another hole in the button. Work in an X-pattern on a four-hole button; make parallel stitches in a two-hole button. Make at least six complete stitches, then wind the thread around the button's stalk three or four times and push the needle through to the back of the fabric. Make a couple of tiny stitches across the thread at the back of the new button, then make a knot and cut the excess thread.

**Fasteners:** Hooks-and-bars are stronger than hooks-and-eyes and snaps because bars hold hooks better than eyes do, and they don't burst open like snap fasteners can. When you buy hooks-and-bars, make sure that they're the right size for the garment. Hooks that are too small will bend and ones that are too large will look clumsy.

**Split Seams:** "Because children grow so quickly, they sometimes wear their clothes too tight," observes Nanny Chadwyck-Healy, who has spent her working life looking after children. "When the seams split, the only thing to do is neatly pin each end of the split with a small safety pin until you can sew it up."

Before you begin sewing, knot the end of the thread. Beginning an inch above

**Sewing Kit Essentials**

Large and small needles
Straight pins
Safety pins
Hooks-and-bars
Small scissors
Seam ripper
Needle threader
Thimble (optional)
Button box
Tape measure
Black thread
White thread
An assortment of colored thread
Iron-on bonding material

## Pulled Threads

Pulled threads are common, especially in the elbows of older knitted garments, where the wool has worn through. Never cut them off. Instead, gently pull the fabric crossways until the loop of thread disappears. Or, you can thread the loose thread onto a needle, bring it to the inside of the garment, and knot it.

## Stopping Runs

To stop a run in nylon hose, apply colorless nail polish or a smear of soap to the end of the run.

the place where the seam is open, follow the line of existing stitch marks. End an inch below the end of the opening, and finish off with a knot.

**Darning Holes:** Always use thread or yarn that's as close in color and texture as possible to the item you're fixing. Many sweaters come with a card of matching darning wool — keep that card in your sewing kit so you can find it when you need it.

**1.** Turn the garment inside out and work in a vertical direction first. Beginning two or three stitches away from the hole, weave the darning thread in and out of the stitches on either side of the hole, making a single long stitch over the hole itself and continuing for two or three stitches beyond the hole. The stitches you make should nearly touch each other. Don't pull them tight — the repaired area should be flexible.

**2.** When you have covered the hole vertically, work horizontally across it, beginning and ending about three inches away from the hole. Weave in and out until the hole is filled. There's no need to finish off.

You can do the same thing to reinforce an area that has become thin but hasn't yet worn through.

**Patching:** Patches are easy to use and work well on holes, tears, and areas that have worn thin. Small patches are nearly invisible, especially when you have carefully cut the patching material from a seam or facing inside the garment you plan to repair. Iron-on patches of various sizes and shapes can be used to mend everything from cigarette burns to tears. Always round the edges of any fabric swatch you plan to use as a patch so it lies smoothly.

**Iron-On Patches:** "Repair specialists used to sew patches," recalls Sava Rasic Harris, "but that's become old-fashioned. Nowadays, most professionals use an iron-on bonding material that holds patches in place even during washing and dry cleaning. (You can buy iron-on bonding material in any housewares or department store.) An ironed-on patch is inconspicuous because it has no stitches and lies flatter than sewn-on patches."

To iron on patches yourself, simply turn the garment inside-out, position the patch on the garment, place the bonding material over it, and then iron. Never let the bonding material come into direct contact with the iron or ironing surface — you can cover the bonding material with brown parcel paper which can be peeled off when you're through. The heat penetrates the bonding material and fuses the patch to the garment. It's important to follow the instructions that come with the bonding material to make sure that the heat needed to iron it on isn't too hot for the clothes you plan to repair. You can also buy colored patches that can be ironed directly on to a garment, either on the inside or the outside, without using bonding material.

If you use leather or suede patches to mend the worn elbows of jackets, make sure they're colorfast. "If they aren't," warns Albert Villenueve, "you'll have to remove the patches every time the item is dry cleaned or the leather will stain the fabric."

**Raincoats:** When seams split in plastic or vinyl-coated rainwear, put the torn edges together so they meet exactly. Hold them in place securely with strips of scotch tape on the outside of the garment. On the inside, cover the tear with one or two wide strips of surgical tape, pressing down firmly. Gently remove the clear tape from the outside. Then sew across the seam from the inside with clear plastic thread. Sew right through the tape from the back — it should not be removed.

## To Unstick a Zipper

Simply rub a soft lead pencil up and down the teeth until the zipper eases. If a zipper won't stay up even though the garment isn't too tight, pull the slider up and pin a small safety pin across the teeth on the inside of the zipper. This will block the slider and hold the zipper closed until you can have it replaced.

Noted author and photographer **James Wagenvoord** has written and/or produced over 40 books, including *The Loving Touch*, *ComputerSpace*, *The Man's Book*, *Making Room*, *The Doubleday Wine Companion*, *Pasta & Cheese: The Cookbook*, *Hangin' Out* and *City Lives*. His work has been published in *Family Circle*, *Redbook*, *Cosmopolitan*, the *New York Times Magazine*, *Penthouse*, and *Vogue*.

**Fiona St. Aubyn** has been writing and contributing to books since the success of her first book, *The Butler's Guide*, in 1980. It was written with Stanley Ager, who for 30 years was butler to her grandparents at St. Michaels' Mount, a castle off the Cornish coast of England. She has contributed to books published by *The Reader's Digest* and was a contributor to *The Doubleday Wine Companion*. She is the author of *London: A Georgian Portrait*.